*Seeking a*
# Research-Ethics Covenant
*in the Social Sciences*

Will C. van den Hoonaard

*Seeking a*
# Research-Ethics Covenant
*in the Social Sciences*

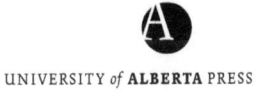
UNIVERSITY *of* ALBERTA PRESS

*Published by*

University of Alberta Press
1-16 Rutherford Library South
11204 89 Avenue NW
Edmonton, Alberta, Canada  T6G 2J4
amiskwaciwâskahikan | Treaty 6 |
Métis Territory
uap.ualberta.ca | uapress@ualberta.ca

Copyright © 2023 Will C. van den Hoonaard
Copyright © 2023 Marco Marzano (Chapter 5: Sociology and the New Ethics Disorder)

*Library and Archives Canada Cataloguing in Publication*

Title: Seeking a research-ethics covenant
    in the social sciences / Will C.
    van den Hoonaard.
Names: Van den Hoonaard, Will. C.
    (Willy Carl), 1942– author.
Description: Includes bibliographical
    references and index.
Identifiers:
    Canadiana (print) 20220481202 |
    Canadiana (ebook) 20220481229 |
    ISBN 9781772126549 (softcover) |
    ISBN 9781772126969 (EPUB) |
    ISBN 9781772126976 (PDF)
Subjects: LCSH: Social sciences—Research—
    Moral and ethical aspects. | LCSH:
    Medicine—Research—Influence.
Classification: LCC H62 .V36 2023 |
    DDC 300.72—dc23

First edition, first printing, 2023.
First printed and bound in Canada by
Houghton Boston Printers, Saskatoon,
Saskatchewan.
Copyediting by Julie Sedivy.
Proofreading by Mary Lou Roy.
Indexing by Stephen Ullstrom.

All rights reserved. No part of this publication may be reproduced, stored in a retrieval system, or transmitted in any form or by any means (electronic, mechanical, photocopying, recording, or otherwise) without prior written consent. Contact University of Alberta Press for further details.

University of Alberta Press supports copyright. Copyright fuels creativity, encourages diverse voices, promotes free speech, and creates a vibrant culture. Thank you for buying an authorized edition of this book and for complying with the copyright laws by not reproducing, scanning, or distributing any part of it in any form without permission. You are supporting writers and allowing University of Alberta Press to continue to publish books for every reader.

This book has been published with the help of a grant from the Canadian Federation for the Humanities and Social Sciences, through the Awards to Scholarly Publications Program, using funds provided by the Social Sciences and Humanities Research Council of Canada.

University of Alberta Press gratefully acknowledges the support received for its publishing program from the Government of Canada, the Canada Council for the Arts, and the Government of Alberta through the Alberta Media Fund.

 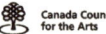

*I dedicate this work to my love, Deborah.*

# Contents

- ix   Preface
- xiii   Acknowledgements

- 1   1 | The Climate of Research-Ethics Review in the Social Sciences

- 21   2 | A Robust Audit Culture and Its Aversion to Diversity

- 31   3 | The Capture of the Social Sciences by the Medical Ethics Framework

- 47   4 | The Anthropological Stance in Ethical Research

- 57   5 | Sociology and the New Ethics Disorder
  *Marco Marzano*

- 69   6 | Current Debates in the Research-Ethics Community

- 87   7 | Towards a New Approach in the Social Sciences

- 107   Appendix: *The New Brunswick Declaration on Research Ethics, Integrity, and Governance*
- 115   Notes
- 119   References
- 139   Index

# Preface

MY OWN MEANDERING through the landscape of research ethics has yielded many surprises. Between 2001 and 2005, I served on the Interagency Panel on Research Ethics (PRE) and its subsidiary, the consultative group of the Social Sciences and Humanities Research Council, work that proved to be a key period in my journey. My written and oral presentations helped me to navigate this landscape, either affirming my initial insights or giving rise to new ones. This output is contained in five books (this volume is my fifth to address research ethics), 34 chapters in other books or refereed articles in handbooks, encyclopedias, and scholarly journals, and an additional 52 formal or informal presentations at conferences or in classrooms.

I began with a perspective about ethics in research that was rather innocent of the larger disciplinary issues that intrude into that landscape. As I moved through that landscape, I soon became aware of how the framework of biomedical ethics had become by far the dominant part of that landscape, unaffected, it seems, by the passage of time, experience, and by the many concerns of researchers in the social sciences and humanities. The Panel on Research Ethics touted the *Tri-Council Policy Statement: Ethical Conduct for Research Involving Humans* (Canadian Institutes of Health Research (CIHR) et al. 2014)—which will henceforth be referred to as *TCPS*—as "a living document." One presumes that this document will continue to change over time, as is reflected in the 2018 version, known as *TCPS* 2 (CIHR et al. 2018).

With the rise of research-ethics review in Canada and elsewhere, I quickly ascertained one of the major threats to social research, namely the dominance of the medical model of ethical research. Soon, I warned my colleagues of an emerging moral panic that had seized the community of researchers in the social sciences (van den Hoonaard 2001), of the fallacy of increased privacy protections around the world that have made research less transparent, of the threats to academic freedom (2006a), of the neo-liberal basis of research-ethics review regimes (2004b), of the overbearing influence of US policies that are dictating research-ethics policies around the world (2006b), and of the role of anglophone countries in setting the bar for ethical research elsewhere in the world (2004b).

As former Chair of the Social Sciences and Humanities Research Ethics Special Working Committee, I was privileged to draft a new chapter (Chapter Ten) in the *TCPS* that focused on research ethics in the social sciences. What struck me afterwards, as a devoted qualitative researcher, was how inadequately the *TCPS* addressed ethical issues in qualitative research. I worked those deep concerns into *Walking the Tightrope* (van den Hoonaard 2002). I also quickly became aware of how researchers in the social sciences faced obstacles in university ethics committees, either because they encountered difficulties in fitting their research into the medical framework or because committees did not fully grasp the approach taken by researchers in the social sciences. My books *The Seduction of Ethics* (2011), *The Ethics Rupture* (van den Hoonaard and Hamilton 2016), and *Walking the Tightrope* (van den Hoonaard 2002), along with "The Ethics Trapeze," a special issue of the *Journal of Academic Ethics* (van den Hoonaard 2006b) I edited, spoke of these dilemmas. My growing awareness of these issues led me to summon many social scientists to convene at a 2012 summit at the University of New Brunswick in Fredericton. There were others like me (van den Hoonaard 2013d) who, on the occasion of that 2012 "Ethics Rupture" summit, were part of a collective effort to highlight the importance of recognizing the special place of the social sciences, while also trying to create smoother relations between ethics committees and researchers.

Following this summit, I began to realize more acutely the degree to which ethics committees had failed to accord respect towards researchers in the social sciences. The summit strongly urged ethics committees to have a fundamental respect for all researchers. The resulting document, *The New Brunswick Declaration on Research Ethics, Integrity, and Governance*, acknowledged the urgent need to recognize research diversity and reflexivity (see Appendix; also van den Hoonaard 2013a; 2014b). In Ivor Gontcharov's (2013) elucidation of the eventual 2013 *New Brunswick Declaration*, obligation is placed squarely upon research-ethics committees to respect and honour the intentions of researchers.

With the participation of so many researchers in the social sciences, word quickly spread that other researchers were also dissatisfied with the hegemony of biomedical ethics. There was an abundance of other voices. Although not organized as a formal global bloc of researchers, bonds of communication that involved the sharing of common concerns became quite evident. I estimate that the number of books and articles that supported the vision of reforms in research-ethics practices probably grew to some 1,000 items, with some 40 to 50 scholars engaged in that struggle.

This volume, *Seeking a Research-Ethics Covenant in the Social Sciences*, expresses the failure of the research-ethics machinery to take our divergent views into account. The book not only elucidates what we can learn from Indigenous perspectives on research ethics, but also sends one important signal: it advocates the use of a covenant in research ethics as a deeply held value in the hearts and minds of researchers.

The current climate of research-ethics review is still based on the medical model of doing ethical research. It is entirely out of step with the nature and processes aligned with doing social research. *Seeking a Research-Ethics Covenant* aims to find a remedy that is satisfactory for researchers in the social sciences.

# Acknowledgements

**EVERYONE APPARENTLY READS** the Acknowledgements. The scope of my gratitude goes far beyond the usual circle of colleagues and friends. In hindsight, I owe a particular debt to ethics committees in Canada (and elsewhere). The decisions of some of these committees have irritated me beyond measure, but that irritation has nevertheless invigorated my own thinking about ethics in research—often leading to conclusions that are the opposite of what the committee members held to be true. I am, however, forced to admit that their motivation is a deep concern about doing research ethically. I also need to acknowledge Canada's Panel on Research Ethics, which I had the honour of serving in an official capacity as Chair of the Task Force on Qualitative Research. That work spurred me to engage in related issues of ethics in research. After my departure from their midst, I continued to experience the support and kindness of panel members in many ways, despite my emerging protests about the dictation of ethics in the social sciences by the medical research-ethics framework.

There is a long slew of scholars who encouraged me along this rocky path of disquiet. Many of their names appear in the bibliography of this volume. My own collection of articles, represented in this bibliography and in those of other scholars, numbers nearly 900.

Around the world, very many scholars offered the kind of critical encouragement and advice every scholar feels obligated to give—and I am grateful for that. Some will not fully agree with my perspectives but I am thankful for all your advice and insights offered along the way: Ann Hamilton, Barbara Clogg-Wright, Brian Martin, Carl Schneider, Catherine Stinson, Cristina Gavrilovici, Deborah Poff, Douglas Wassenaar, Dvora Yanow, Iara

Guerriero, Ivor Gontcharov, Janice Mary Ryan, Joan Sieber, Julie Bull, the late Kathy Charmaz, Lisa Wynn, Mark Israel, Martin Tolich, Martyn Hammersley, Michael Goodyear, Nathan Emmerich, Patti and Peter Adler, Rena Lederman, Robert Dingwall, Ron Glass, Ron Iphofen, Rosa Castillo, Ted Palys, Simon Whitney, Steven Kleinknecht, Zachary Schrag, Peter Weeks, and Zelda Doyle. In particular, I need to recognize the generous contributions of two scholars, namely Julie Bull and Marco Marzano. Both Julie and Marco are steadfast friends and colleagues whose ideas on Indigenous research-ethics and sociology, respectively, carry an enormous appeal. I also extend my thanks to Mat Buntin, Acquisitions Editor at University of Alberta Press, for his prompt and steady flow of advice regarding *Seeking a Research-Ethics Covenant in the Social Sciences*. To Julie Sedivy, I wish to express my heartfelt gratitude for her sterling contributions as copy editor, which have extended beyond any normal range of her work. Her zeal included offering encouragement, advice, copious notes and queries, and she helped me to visualize the final leg of the book's journey.

I can never fully express my gratitude for being surrounded by a personal family of scholars: Deborah van den Hoonaard, Cheryl Power, Gabriel Power, Jeff van den Scott, Jordan van den Hoonaard, Lisa-Jo van den Scott, and Morgan van den Hoonaard—sociologist, educator, economist, musicologist, philosopher, sociologist, and public relations practitioner. Each one of you has contributed your share of insights and loving encouragement.

I strongly suspect, though, that my wife, Deborah, who has her own impeccable record of scholarly achievements as a sociologist/gerontologist, was fated to bear the brunt of the overwrought dedication of a husband whose whole goal was to finally address the wrongs of ethic policies. Using the strategies of eye-rolling good humour, a steadfast belief in my work, and unquestioned support, she carried me through many publications on top of her own meritorious work. She exemplifies the person who is unstinting in her support and knows a thing or two about how to instill in me a desire to conduct good research. It must not be easy to suffer her husband's obsession with a particular research topic. I dedicate this volume to her.

# 1
## *The Climate of* Research-Ethics Review
### *in the Social Sciences*

AS AN UNDERGRADUATE, I recall taking honours courses in anthropological linguistics, working on a Wolastoqiyik (Maliseet) dictionary. These courses familiarized me with strategies for doing fieldwork and allowed me to become acquainted with Indigenous research approaches.[1] Following this period, Dr. Raoul R. Andersen, an anthropologist at Memorial University of Newfoundland, offered to supervise my anthropological fieldwork in a small fishing village on Iceland's southern coast (van den Hoonaard 1972). Learning Icelandic was part of that fieldwork experience. My next fieldwork experience (this time in Northwest Iceland in another fishing area, conducted under the aegis of Dr. Anthony P. Cohen, a social anthropologist at the University of Manchester in England), solidified my love and interest in doing anthropological research and fieldwork. After I completed my academic studies, I continued to do research, including work on the Dutch of New Brunswick (van den Hoonaard 1991), historical research on the Bahá'í people of Canada (1996), and a 700-year history of women in cartography (2013c). All of this research entailed personal interviews, participant observation, and attendance at gatherings. These varied research activities led me to author books, publish articles, and edit scholarly works. I imbibed lessons on research ethics while acquainting myself with empirical literature that dotted the landscape of the social sciences.

The title of Rebecca Solnit's book, *A Paradise Built in Hell* (2009) inspired me to observe that many seemingly ideal efforts, such as creating national and international research-ethics codes, incorporate negative elements that run counter to the ideals which spurred these efforts. In the experience of researchers in the social sciences, that idealistic paradise has indeed turned into a hell as a result of unsuccessful attempts to apply research-ethics principles in medicine to their own research trade.

*Seeking a Research-Ethics Covenant in the Social Sciences* demonstrates the failure of current ethics codes to serve as meaningful tools for researchers in the social sciences. Many, especially researchers in the social sciences, find that this failure has had a disordering and disorienting effect on their research as a result of policy makers inappropriately imposing the "order" of biomedical research upon the social sciences.

Four pillars sustain the disorder that pervades contemporary ethics practices in the social sciences: (a) an aggressive audit culture that pervades universities; (b) the privileged status of the medical research-ethics framework; (c) the capture by that framework of the social sciences; and (d) the divergent complaints and analyses among researchers in the social sciences, resulting in conflicting perspectives about how to remedy problems in current ethics codes. All these pillars serve to undercut active research in the social sciences. In particular, the dominance of the medical research-ethics framework makes it difficult for researchers in the social sciences to make the case that their approach to research is based on equally valid ethical principles. As a corollary, research-ethics committees, relying on the medical framework to make decisions, usually invalidate approaches in the social sciences.

Researchers around the world have tried to tackle this dilemma (and I and Marco Marzano will consider these attempts later in the book). At the time of writing, researchers need to bend or orient their research around inflexible rules that have no bearing on the realities of doing ethical social-science research. Currently, many researchers in the social sciences are regarded as ethics nihilists or as naive when it comes to ethics in research.

Paradoxically, ethics regulations have actually led many researchers not to pay credence to the formal rules of ethics. *Seeking a Research-Ethics Covenant* hopes to offer a new perspective on solving the ongoing ethics disorder. It argues that, given the failure of current structures, researchers in the social sciences should adopt the idea of a research-ethics covenant, a coherent model of ethics in research that can occupy a hallowed space in the hearts and minds of researchers. The book implores researchers to adopt a covenantal approach to achieve a measure of hope and progress in research ethics.

This book suggests we move away from the conventional ethics framework—to forgo it, in fact. *Seeking a Research-Ethics Covenant* will unravel the main features that led to the current situation, namely (as mentioned above) the rise of audit culture, the privilege accorded to the medical framework of ethical research, and the inability on the part of many of us researchers in the social sciences to credibly counter the medical framework of ethics and create viable alternatives. The current state of research-ethics codes highlights the need for fresh approaches to conducting ethical research. Marginalized communities around the world have experienced obstacles in working with the prevailing medically based ethics framework. Fortunately, a number of these communities, such as various Indigenous peoples in Canada (see, *e.g.*, Bull 2010; 2019) and the Māori in New Zealand (Hudson and Russell 2009) have already put forward alternative models that demonstrate that change is possible. I present the case of Indigenous peoples not only to show that it is possible to break out of the cage of the framework based on medical ethics, but also to warm the heart of reader by illustrating how such changes can indeed be vast and meaningful. These examples serve as the background to my own proposal, which focuses on the use of a research-ethics covenant. The rising body of Indigenous research and praxis is highly promising and closely interwoven with the lives of Indigenous researchers and communities.

During my long, informal—and sometimes formal—association with First Nations groups in Canada spanning almost 60 years, I became acquainted with some Indigenous outlooks on research. It was therefore quite natural for me to take note of Indigenous perspectives on ethics in the early 2000s, at a time when I was also engaged in developing ideas on that topic.

My first association with an Indigenous community began in 1966, when I responded to a personal invitation to visit a Tłı̨chǫ (Dogrib) home in Yellowknife, Northwest Territories. During my early years in university between 1967 and 1970, I was fortunate to have witnessed the nurturing of artistic talent among First Nations youth in New Brunswick and to have participated in the creation of a Wolastoqiyik (Maliseet) dictionary as part of a two-year project initiated by the Human Rights Commission of New Brunswick under the tutelage of Walter Joe Paul in Sitansisk Wolastoqiyik (St. Mary's First Nation) in Fredericton. During this time, with the encouragement of an Elder at Pilick (Kingsclear) First Nation, I was also permitted to involve some 60 university students in helping primary-school children in the community do their homework.

In 1979, upon my subsequent return to academic work at the University of New Brunswick after working as an alternate representative of an NGO at the United Nations in New York City, I was invited to teach a sociology class at the Eskasoni First Nation on Cape Breton Island, where my children attended classes. Much later one of my daughters and her husband stayed in one of the most remote places in Canada's Arctic region, where she involved young girls in various crafts; when my daughter and son-in-law decided to undertake a study there, my heart sang with admiration for their efforts. After five years in Arviat, the local Council of Elders gave them permission to share their research findings with others.

In the early 2010s, when I had the honour of being invited to serve as the external reader for the defense of Julie Bull's PhD dissertation on ethics in research, I acquitted myself to that task to the best of my abilities. Julie Bull has found her calling as a researcher, artist, and poet. She is a NunatuKavut (Southern Inuk) woman with familial ties to Paradise River in Sandwich Bay on the southeastern coast of Labrador. (She grew up partially on the island of Newfoundland and in central Labrador. Most of her immediate and extended family still lives in central and southern Labrador). Julie is a researcher who has been actively involved with articulating themes related to research ethics, community-driven research, Indigenous methodologies, and Arctic research. A summary of her ideas in her 2010 article offers the specific new insights that Indigenous methodologies bring to the conversation about research ethics. She claims that authenticity is the "precursor" to ethical research, and that is "how communities and researchers collaborate together in a co-learning environment whereby mutual interests and agendas are discussed and enacted in the entire research process" (Bull 2010:19). As a consequence, "trust becomes paramount." In this context, nurturing a research-ethics covenant becomes the key point. More fundamental than a mechanical checklist defining ethical research is the idea of how the research embodies authentic relationships and trust (see also van den Scott 2018).

The central problem with current ethics practices is a disconnection between ideologies or theories of how to conduct ethical research and the mechanistic practice of conducting ethical research. As we might anticipate, in Indigenous research-ethics practices, the narrative is quite different. From the outset, the earliest draft of the *TCPS*—the *Tri-Council Policy Statement: Ethical Conduct for Research Involving Humans* (CIHR et al. 2014)—dedicated a full chapter (Chapter Nine) to Indigenous research. This recognition of the value of Indigenous research predates the 94 Calls to Action of the Truth and Reconciliation Commission (TRC) of Canada. The TRC lodged its concerns about Indigenous research as part of a process of reconciliation between Canadians and Indigenous peoples, a process that was prompted by the recognition of the assimilationist role of the Indian residential schools system and its educational institutions and their role in cultural genocide. A handful of recommendations in the TRC *Calls to Action* (2015) offer Indigenous-relevant research approaches. We should bear in mind that Indigenous researchers have not had the opportunity to inculcate public knowledge of relevant Indigenous research until very recently. Nonetheless, one can see how some of the TRC's recommendations can be interpreted as promulgating Indigenous research approaches. More specifically, the TRC *Calls to Action* provide some useful suggestions. These include developing culturally appropriate curricula (TRC 2015:10.iii); providing education to public servants on the history of Indigenous peoples and requiring skills-based training in intercultural competency (TRC 2015:57); providing the necessary funding to post-secondary institutions to educate teachers on how to integrate Indigenous knowledge and teaching methods into classrooms (TRC 2015:62.ii); establishing senior-level positions in government at the assistant deputy minister level or higher dedicated to Indigenous content in education (TRC 2015:62.iv); building student capacity for intercultural understanding, empathy, and mutual respect (TRC 2015:63.iii); establishing a national research program to advance understanding of reconciliation (TRC 2015:65); and requiring medical and nursing schools to provide skills-based training in intercultural competency, conflict resolution, human rights, and anti-racism (TRC 2015:24). It can be clearly seen that the overarching demand is to create the means for bringing about intercultural competency. Any effort to direct a researcher's gaze to the particular characteristics of doing ethical research in accordance with Indigenous principles would be a most welcome response to that summons.

The early foundational work of the *TCPS* led researchers, both Indigenous and others, to recognize that social-science research had colonized Indigenous research. However, increasingly, the values and characteristics of Indigenous approaches in Canada are permeating current perspectives on research ethics among many scholars, Indigenous and settler alike. These emerging perspectives remain at the heart of doing research with Indigenous peoples (First Nations, Inuit, and Métis Nations) and contain many insights that may be of significant help to many other researchers, even those around the world, who are dissatisfied with the medicalized approach to research ethics that is currently mandated. At the risk of making undue generalizations when distilling these perspectives from just one or a few Indigenous researchers, one has no choice but to seek shade under the umbrella of some Indigenous researcher. For example, in my own work (van den Hoonaard 2014a), I have drawn on Linda Tuhiwai Smith's (1999) book *Decolonizing Methodologies: Research and Indigenous Peoples*. Throughout *Seeking a Research-Ethics Covenant,* I have relied on Julie Bull's 2010 and 2019 works, which provide the kinds of insights we can all potentially use in conducting ethical research.

Instead of research *on* or *about* Indigenous people, one conducts research *with* Indigenous people, the latter leading the research rather than merely serving as subjects. Every researcher must see such an effort as "an invitation for researchers to think, know and act differently" (Bull 2019:ii). What needs to be underscored is that such research should aim to simultaneously decolonize and Indigenize the research. Even an initial exploration of existing research demonstrates an "incongruence in research ethics and it is particularly evident in the practice of research/review with Indigenous Peoples" (Bull 2019:iv). It is already evident that one's place in the larger context of family, as conceptualized by doing research *with* an Indigenous population, means that researchers need to direct their gaze not only to decolonize research but also to see that research ethics constitutes the earliest step in such research. A paradigm shift is already occurring in health research involving Indigenous peoples. What is more, according to Bull, both Indigenous communities and academia "are required to work together to address an issue...highlighting the necessity of integration." (Bull 2019:2). Roger Poole has articulated the notion of an ethical space in which engagement is essential in conducting health research involving Indigenous peoples (Poole 1972). Mi'kmaw Elders Albert and Murdena Marshall[2] later articulated *Etuaptmumk* (Two-Eyed Seeing) as "integrating both Western and Indigenous Science in a co-learning model" (Bull 2019:2).

An important part of the movement for ethical conduct and review of research with Indigenous peoples is teaching the importance of locating oneself in the research (Absolon 2011; Moore 2015). Reflexivity is a *requirement* in Indigenous research, regardless of the discipline or subject matter, because Indigenous research is relational. "Locating self is always necessary in research with Indigenous Peoples" avers Bull (2019:5–6), "no matter the context—whether we are at home welcoming others to our territory, visiting another Indigenous territory, or meeting on non-Indigenous territories or with non-Indigenous people." Bull informs us that when she introduces herself, she does so in relationship to her familial and territorial connections. She stresses the importance of reflexivity in research/review with Indigenous peoples by locating herself in this research. Similarly, another scholar (Smith

2020) asserts that relationality is integral, and we need to be able to articulate our location to others.

It is no surprise to realize that "our identities are in constant flux and are impacted by the relationships we have with the people and social worlds around us and our relationships with the wider world shape these identities" (Bull 2019:12). We learn from Julie Bull (2019:12) that "[c]ritical self-reflection in the pursuit of deep understanding is centered in the work" she does and "reflects a tenet of Indigenous research practices globally; this approach ensures [she] take[s] time to evaluate [herself] in *relationship* to the research" (see also: Martin 2012; Sium and Ritskes 2013).

Both passion and research integrity are a part of Julie Bull's work as a scholar. What follows is her own approach, which other Indigenous researchers do not necessarily share. I describe her approach below as an example of how an Indigenous researcher walks the difficult path of avoiding losing herself in the relatively new land of academia. Julie Bull describes "a demonstration of 'the dance' that many Indigenous scholars find themselves in as they navigate meeting everyone's expectations (in communities and at institutions) to be responsible researchers" (Bull 2019:14).

She speaks of resorting to the *Spirit Voice*, which "speaks when there are relevant stories of challenge, discomfort, guidance, validation, confirmation, and direction. To spiritually engage with the work means to be present. To be brave. To be humble. To be grateful. It is to learn to sit in discomfort. To learn to trust. It is to make the assertion that 'I have to believe it to see it' rather than 'I have to see it to believe it'" (Bull 2019:7). She also evokes her *Personal Voice*. That voice adumbrates self-reflection, "but in places where [she has] inserted [her] most personal stories." She integrates her *Poetic Voice* throughout her account, a voice that is "instrumental in [her] becoming an 'able human'" (Bull 2019:8). Finally, she employs the *Academic Voice* where "academics will feel most at ease, in their natural environment."

It stands to reason that Bull, not unlike other Indigenous researchers, is attracted to (auto) ethnography when doing ethical research with Indigenous peoples. Mariza Méndez, a colleague at the University of Manchester, has expressed a similar point in a paper in the *Colombian Applied Linguistics Journal*:

> [T]he richness of autoethnography is in those realities [or deep understandings] that emerge from the interaction between the self and its own experiences that reflect the cultural and social context in which those events took place. (Méndez 2013:284)

One major cultural element of Indigenous peoples' experiences of academic institutions is that they "rarely find themselves in scenarios where black-and-white thinking is useful or practical; Indigenous scholars often hold several spaces and places simultaneously, and rarely can fit their entire selves in the artificial insider-outsider binary 'box' where objectivity supposedly lives" (Bull 2019:14).

Reliance on relational processes is "the strongest theme in... Indigenous research ethics" at "every stage of the research—from the researchers' own intentions in seeking particular knowledge, through the design and implementation of methodologies and gathering of consent, to the analysis and dissemination of knowledge" (Riddell et al. 2017, quoted in Bull 2019:30). However, Julie Bull (2019:2) is the first to admit that "[w]hile the notion of doing research *with* people sounds simple, simplicity does not follow in practice." Many detailed policies have "led to apprehensions and misinterpretations between institutional research ethics review and Indigenous community research review." Those doing ethical Indigenous research may have trouble negotiating with research-ethics boards (REBs) on how to define an ethical space that operates from a position of *Etuaptmumk* (Two-Eyed Seeing). We might still be a long way off from elevating Indigenous research authority and implementing an Indigenous governance structure within the REB system.

In discussing Indigenous research-ethics here, my intent is to open up the possibility of the existence of other perspectives, loosening the seemingly inevitable mould of the medical research-ethics paradigm. The notion of a research-ethics covenant (as advocated in this volume) may prove to be one of most viable ways of overcoming the perplexing dilemmas that face anyone doing Indigenous research. Such researchers, according to Bull,

> [oscillate] between multiple worlds where epistemologies, ontologies, and methodologies sometimes overlap/conflict, where local priorities reflect/reject research agendas or priority funding announcements, where Indigenous knowledges are becoming visible/invisible within academic health research, where complex governance structures are challenged/influenced by globally significant and locally specific events, where health disparities persist, in spite of/despite (misplaced) efforts to address them, where collective consent is prescribed the same process as individual consent, and where communities, researchers, and REBs are left unsure how to proceed responsibly against a complex historical and ongoing backdrop of colonialism and inequality. (Bull 2019:266)

While I consider the imposition of a Western academic model of science on Indigenous research to be a form of "colonization," I suggest that the imposition of a medical research-ethics framework constitutes "capture." The concept of colonization or dictation defines an intricate social, economic, and political process. Capture denotes a more straightforward process whereby a way of doing things has become a legal requirement, imposed without the benefit of fully assessing its negative consequences. Adopting a research-ethics covenant will go a long way to alleviate the problems inherent in the biomedical approach to ethics in research. No specifically mandated codes can capture the essence of ethical behaviour for researchers in the non-medical sciences. My intent in discussing Indigenous research strategies is to show that change is possible and, in fact, quite inevitable in the arena of research ethics. Nothing stays the same. The promulgation of knowledge about Indigenous research epistemologies and practices is a clarion call that change is possible. The covenant's emphasis on reflective thinking, the obligation for researchers to educate themselves, the discovery of ethical knowledge according to wider social contexts and relevant practices, including input from Elders, positive contributions from communities, and a constructive engagement with the community and research participants can "bring together the culmination of the teachings" (Bull 2019:vii).

As Julie Bull (2019:269) has so eloquently pointed out, "asserting and assessing levels of community/Indigenous engagement through paper-driven REB processes continues to fail researchers and communities and may be failing REBs too as they navigate matters of institutional liability alongside research trustworthiness and ethics." Bull offers a compelling (and poetic) stance:

> The intricate weaving of humankind and human relationships is not meant to be disentangled, it is meant to be embraced, explored, examined, and lived. We can learn from the intricacies of the interconnectedness, rather than attempt to ignore it or unravel it with futility. It is here in this place, in this time in the story that we can begin to understand the *ethical space*...Ethics is not something that exists outside of ourselves. It is within us and throughout us. I am this duality. (2019:271)

When I first proposed this book, I called for an ethics-review revolution in the social sciences. However, I now believe a more drastic and fundamental orientation towards ethics in research is needed. I realize that it is no small matter to discount the growing universal bureaucratic framework of how to conduct ethical research. It is perhaps too much to hope for a new ethics revolution: the current mix of social, political, and bureaucratic power structures has sustained strong resistance against sweeping change. However, I have no wish to create more stringent ethics rules for research in the social sciences. I have written this book with the goal of freeing the social sciences from the disorder created by a research-ethics review system that is driven by (medical) concepts alien to researchers in the social sciences. This fundamental misalignment is the reason why the few narratives surrounding the alleged ethical failures in social research fall so short of the reality of social research. Typically, a review of the so-called ethical "failures" in the social sciences implicates informed consent, deception, privacy (including confidentiality and anonymity), or physical or mental distress (Hilton *et al.* 2019). These issues pertain more to research in psychology—not to those relevant in ethnographic or community-wide research, or to sociological explorations of communities or other human collectivities.

A cursory view of ethical practices in the social sciences prior to the establishment of the current ethics codes reveals a rather superficial approach, one that mixed formal lessons from biomedical research with lessons gained in the aftermath of such geopolitical convulsions as the American experience in wars in Vietnam and other parts of the world. The Canadian edition of a major introductory textbook on sociology (Macionis *et al.* 1994) provides a typical approach. The textbook contains a 500-word statement on research ethics that reveals two sources for ethical reflection, namely the biomedical paradigm and the lessons apparently gathered from the United States' involvement in conflict around the world. From the biomedical paradigm, the textbook urges sociologists to be technically competent and objective, to disclose their findings in full, to include all possible interpretations of the data, to make those results known to qualified sociologists, to strive to protect the rights, privacy, and safety of the research participants, to make participants aware if the research may cause discomfort or cause risk, and to entitle them to full anonymity. From the experiences of American sociologists involved in conflict zones worldwide, the following solemn declarations have arisen: sociologists are bound to present accurately the purpose of their work, must inform research participants if sociologists represent political or business organizations, must never accept funding from organizations that will constrain the research, must disclose all sources of research funding, must never use their cover as sociologists to gather information for any government, and must gain familiarity with the local setting to understand in advance people's notion of privacy or source of personal danger.

The history of ethical conceptualization in anthropology seems strikingly different from that of sociology. Initially, anthropology's principal ethical stance was to cultivate a sensitivity and understanding of the cultures being studied. The latest manifestation of the anthropologist's ethical obligations entails negotiating *both* with the people involved and with the sponsors of anthropological research. Thus, one ventures to hope that the social sciences can expand the sphere of research ethics beyond the domains of biomedical research. What has complicated any consideration of ethical research in the social sciences is the seeming evaporation of specific ethical guidance for the social sciences. What policy makers have left us is a mandated ethics system based on biomedical research.

Wrestling with ideas takes time. This book took eighteen years to take hold. Along the way, many have travelled this path with me and I owe them deep gratitude. Their commitment to ethics as well as their formal and personal encouragement were clear signs that they wanted to see the best ethical practices put into place. However, eventually the worldwide official embrace of medical research ethics became the dominant theme in universities and in government circles. The capture by medical ethics regimes around the world has, however, given researchers in the social sciences an opportunity to think more deeply about what they can offer to the world that is at variance with the biomedical ethics regimes. Unfortunately, many researchers in the social sciences encountered a sea of turmoil and graceless opposition as they tried to articulate research-ethics ideas they believed were more in tune with the exigencies of the social sciences. Researchers in the social sciences, however, are not ethics nihilists. What is now clear is the realization that all we need to do is to breathe in the practices and wisdoms we have accrued throughout decades of social-science research.

A universe of ethical principles resides within our work as social scientists; it is not something we need to extract from the biomedical atmosphere that dominates institutional committees. Those ethics principles are, however, currently hidden in a labyrinth of studies in our discipline, or sometimes buried in a modest footnote. We cannot discover them on the fly. This can make it seem easier, perhaps even more helpful, to distill ethical practices from the medical framework of research ethics that has publicly and formally been promulgated around the world as a panacea for all the challenging questions posed by ethics in research. Like a vortex, the medical framework threatens to pull all of us into believing that there are no substantial ethical facets that exist outside of that framework.

Lest the reader believes that the social sciences disavow ethics in research, the actual theme of this book is about gaining a deeper appreciation of a new mode of thinking that requires us to reflect on the value and significance of Indigenous research, the evolution of ethics in anthropology, and the acute dilemmas facing social science when its ethics practices are restricted to the medical research-ethics codes. My goal is to demonstrate the value of adhering to a research-ethics covenant.

The difficulty of finding an alternative model for the social sciences originates from within the ranks of researchers themselves. Many lack conscious knowledge of genuine ethical precepts in the social sciences or have simply adopted the biomedical framework as their own. In this manner, they have "othered" themselves (van den Hoonaard 2013b), exemplifying a false disciplinary consciousness. This enables researchers in the biomedical fields to produce the narrative of what "should" constitute social-science research (van den Hoonaard 2006b).

Many scholars may believe that it is not easy to navigate the labyrinth of ethical social research. Who can afford the time and energy to step into that maze and search out those ethical nuggets that lie deep in our history and practice of social research? Is it not easier to muddle through a working relationship with an ethics committee and publicly vow adherence to a biomedical framework that "everyone" has already agreed upon? These external and internal forces have stymied the appreciation of our authentic potential to do ethical research in a manner that would lead to the re-efflorescence of the social sciences. For me, the real and genuine surprise was the discovery that agencies working to create an ethics framework have ignored the principles of ethical research in the social sciences, barely touching upon them. We cannot blame these agencies. After all, we researchers in the social sciences were barely able to find our way through our own ethics labyrinth.

As my colleague Ron Iphofen reminded me via email on March 27, 2020, we need to mark a distinction between ethics-review *processes* (which vary in extremes) and ethical research *practices* (which vary in application and need). We must also remember the difference between *governance* and *ethics* and the need to separate issues of corporate liability from the oversight of ethical research itself. The term *governance* sounds so concrete and immovable. It makes one hesitate to embark on any venture that suggests changing or removing it altogether. Whenever such attempts are made, one notes a deep silence on the part of policy makers and those who are entrusted with maintaining the structure of research-ethics review on the issue of governance. One example of such silence can be seen in the fact that those responsible for maintaining ethics governance have not grappled with the meteoric rise of qualitative social research over the past 30 years. Yes, it is true that the Panel on Research Ethics in Canada felt prompted to create a chapter in the *TCPS* 2 (CIHR *et al.* 2018) devoted exclusively to qualitative research (Chapter Ten). However, while many qualitative researchers might be heartened to see a special chapter devoted to ethics in undertakings by qualitative researchers, they may also be discouraged by the various statements in that chapter overriding their own concerns with matters that emphasize the medical ethics framework.

First, Chapter Ten in *TCPS* 2 claims that many divergent fields express a "common belief" in "trying to understand human action through systematic study and analysis" (CIHR *et al.* 2018:Chapter Ten). The use of the terms "systematic study and analysis" signals to ethics committees that they must uphold the quantitative perspective in research. The key value of qualitative research of being inductive, flexible, and context-dependent appears much later in the chapter. Qualitative researchers, however, will fail to see any similarity between anthropology, sociology, and criminology, on one hand, and philosophy, psychology, and business administration, on the other hand. From the perspective of qualitative researchers, only psychology incorporates the essential concepts inherent to a medical research frame.

Second, the numerous references to "health research" in this chapter indicate the current penchant for undertaking that kind of research (it is usually well-funded), but this topic seems far removed from the interest and research of qualitative researchers.

Third, Chapter Ten emphasizes that "[m]any of the research practices and methodological requirements that characterize qualitative research approaches parallel those that characterize quantitative approaches, such as concerns regarding research quality." This statement eliminates significant differences between qualitative and quantitative research, failing to take into account the knowledge that qualitative researchers have gained over the years. On the same page, one also learns that "this chapter seeks to provide specific guidance on some issues that are particularly germane to qualitative research"—but it may come as no surprise to then read: "although such guidance may also be applicable to research using quantitative or mixed methods."

Fourth, the opening paragraphs in this chapter ignore the serious methodological and epistemological problems that qualitative researchers attach to such issues as consent, privacy, and confidentiality, even though the chapter acknowledges that these issues apply "equally in the context of qualitative research." It is clear from this document why ethics committees will see no particular motivation to address ethical issues that are germane to qualitative research. (To be fair, the remaining part of the chapter does do justice to the particular needs of qualitative research, but the opening four paragraphs run counter to that justice.)

Fifth, the references at the end of Chapter Ten contain only formal policy statements regarding privacy, accessing results, integrity, and data archiving. These concerns do not touch the prevailing issues regarding ethics in qualitative research.

It is my impression, however, that many researchers are unaware of how this chapter of *TCPS* 2 actually downplays the particular proclivities of qualitative research (and, by extension, of research in the social sciences in general). Thus, even if they have awareness of the contents of Chapter Ten, research-ethics boards are inclined to resort to the provisions of the *TCPS* that are explicitly medical in orientation. Given the burgeoning growth of scholars engaged in qualitative research, one would have expected comprehensive policy shifts in ethics codes to accommodate the ethical sensibilities that social scientists are used to. There have been no such shifts. That struggle is still ahead of us. Without such a shift away from medical policies, ethical social research will, according to Baggini (2018), become distorted, misguided, and parochial, leading to the entropy of the social sciences themselves.

The rise of capital-intensive research has revalidated the positivistic orientation of the natural sciences. Long-term ethnographic stays in the field run counter to the strong preference among researchers to do as much research as possible in the shortest amount of time. Moreover, research in less-recognized, less-sexy areas does not yield much in the way of citations or other forms of scholarly recognition. Even a full career in the study of widowhood (*e.g.*, D. van den Hoonaard 2001) does not yield the metrics, citations, or wider appreciation of its value compared to, let us say, the quantitative study of economic inequality. The capital-intensive accounting of qualitative research can never do full justice to its value.

The United States Department of Education (2002) has indicated that ethnographic research in topics that do not fall under traditional normative standards should no longer be designated as belonging to a conventional "scientific" agenda; such research should therefore not receive funding. The significant rise of research with a capitalist orientation, driven by capitalist values including efficiency and shareholder value, has created a mighty bulwark against the use of distinctive methodologies and practices in the social sciences. In this vein, Peter Pels (2018b:412) speaks about being very wary of adopting "neoliberal ideologies of transparency." Research within a digital culture, with its insistence on, for example, data transparency, reproduces inequality between social sciences and biomedical sciences. The alleged need to produce research findings as quickly as possible also drives researchers into a climate of competition rather than cooperation. A deep faith in science and technology as a means to reorder the social and natural world reaffirms the idea of conventional research with agreed-upon norms. This denies the growing influence of qualitative research in certain areas.

The vigorous emergence of health research in the social sciences, an area that attracts more substantial research grants than non-health-related research, reinforces the use of positivist research. Many university departments in the social sciences initially welcomed these well-funded health researchers. This is akin to welcoming the Trojan Horse, filled not with

Greek warriors, but with templates to emulate the hypo-deductive methods of positivist research (D. van den Hoonaard 2019). The rise of interdisciplinary research also grew across a variety of university departments, undermining inductive and qualitative research, or including it as part of a "mixed-methods" package.

The time has now come to counteract the dominant influence of the biomedical ethics framework.[3] Lest the reader be left with the notion that I am advocating a full-spectrum destruction of the biomedical framework of ethics, let me emphasize that nothing is further from the truth. If medical researchers and ethics boards find comfort in the application of this framework to clinical or medical research, all well and good. Similarly, political scientists, economists, and researchers in other allied fields will have to find their own paths in the sand. However, the proposals I lay out in this book's final chapter should elicit their interest.

Chapter Two of this volume touches on the growth of audit culture in universities and how the surge of interdisciplinary research has deadened our senses to the unique methodological and conceptual contributions of sociological research. The chapter highlights concerns about doing ethical research that stem from a rather enthusiastic audit culture in universities (and elsewhere). This audit culture ensures that any research under the aegis of a university conforms to a generic ethics template that seems out of place for researchers in the social sciences. Within this culture, the standards of conducting ethical research not only originate in but also promote the biomedical framework of research ethics.

Chapter Two sets out the significant differences between the medical research-ethics framework and that of the social sciences. Despite these important differences between the two fields of research, there is no recognition of them in the audit culture in universities. Unfortunately, it is necessary to bring to light how, despite the loud clamour of researchers in the social sciences, ethics policy makers and others have ignored their concerns. The silence around these concerns creates a lack of confidence about how alternative ideas about research ethics will be received. I am worried that, given its dominant position, the existing audit culture will feel compelled to reject any stance that might argue for alternative models of research ethics. One such alternative model concerns the widely growing interest in how to conduct ethical research with Indigenous peoples and communities.

There are also two special chapters on anthropology and sociology respectively, devoted to the evolution of ethical research practices in these fields before many national ethics codes came into force some 40 years ago.

Dr. Marco Marzano of Bergamo University, Italy, has kindly contributed Chapter Five on the adverse effects of research-ethics review on sociological research. Dr. Marzano is well known in the field of ethics in critical social research. His work vigorously interrogates how to conduct ethical research in an era dominated by forces that threaten qualitative sociological research. His chapter shows that when sociologists follow and rigorously obey the regulatory culture espoused by ethics committees, this has serious implications for sociological research. Such regulatory cultures contravene some of the main principles for doing sociological research, effectively giving up the critical study of the social context and all that is bound up with aspects of the lives of the groups, communities, and organizations we study. According to Marzano, we end up researching only "politically innocuous subjects and people whom researchers consider friends or towards whom they have positive feelings." Settings that involve the prestigious, the powerful, the fate of their victims, and the injustices that occur fall by the wayside. Marzano's chapter is bold in its assertions. He discusses how the invented notion of "harm" or "risk" (which ethics policies warn us about) has damaged the progress of sociological research.

The final two chapters (Six and Seven) spell out the direction of *Seeking a Research-Ethics Covenant*. Chapter Six presents, as fairly as possible, desirable solutions to the dilemma caused by imposing rather irrelevant models on social scientists who have to follow a particular model of ethical research. That chapter discusses the benefits and disadvantages of eight proffered solutions. It presents each proposal in meticulous and carefully researched detail.

Chapter Seven presents a unique solution to our dilemma. Based on the clear thinking of Dr. Rosa Cordillera A. Castillo and others, I urge institutions and researchers to adopt an ethics covenant. I envision in due course that the covenant will represent a series of tutorials where we all explore the ethical dimensions of social research. These are not courses on how to do ethical research, but rather explorations of ethics in social research, along with more explicit presentation of materials already available in universities and other institutions of learning and training. This approach allows research-ethics committees to concentrate on the more specific issues of medical research. In contrast, covenants are solemn instruments of self-direction more suited to research in the social sciences.

*Seeking a Research-Ethics Covenant* outlines both specific and general concerns about research-ethics review that have led many to explore new frameworks—or to abandon them. Throughout this book, I aim to be forthright and reveal my own unease with the current ethics regimes, an unease that comes from my training and experience as a social anthropologist and sociologist.

# 2

## *A Robust* Audit Culture *and Its Aversion to Diversity*

**THIS CHAPTER DEMONSTRATES** the impact of audit culture within universities. An audit culture is premised on the need to assimilate and make sense of the diverse constituent parts of the university. A robust audit culture may appear healthy, but in the experience of researchers in the social sciences who must work through existing ethics codes, that culture is relentless or malignant—a physician might use the term *metastatic*.

Formally reviewing the ethical aspects of research involving humans did not come at the insistence of researchers. Rather, the rise of formal ethics reviews resulted from various sources, all of which were intertwined with governmental efforts to stave off ethical transgressions, first in clinical and medical research, and then in other research undertakings. The first source, a growing audit culture in universities (and elsewhere), paved the way for the formal establishment, in the 1970s, of research-ethics codes that eventually encircled the globe. Privileging the medical research-ethics paradigm was the second development that led to the implementation of national and international ethics codes. The awareness of a series of ethical transgressions in clinical and medical research pushed the acceptance of codes as a rational method to ward off future transgressions. The force of the medical research-ethics paradigm, with its detailed, articulate, and well-defined system of ethics, captured the other disciplines. The third source came from a surprising corner of research, namely the relative weakness, or even the lack of any articulation of ethics codes in the social sciences. Taking into account a wide range of research methods and settings, researchers in the social sciences took their ethical cues from veteran researchers who, in their books and articles as well as in class lectures, took it upon themselves to highlight the ethical challenges and solutions relevant to their research. These ethical teachings were part of the lore and history in the social sciences. With the passage of time, researchers in the social sciences became acutely aware of the ways in which the medical framework of research ethics differed greatly from the ways in which researchers in the social sciences approached their topics. Given that the ethical nuances were so dramatically different from one research topic to another, the formal research-ethics codes were not able to absorb this radical diversity. To policy makers, the clamour of researchers in the social sciences must have sounded like a cacophony of various ideas, wide-ranging criticisms, and contradictory solutions. Audit culture is ultimately hostile to diversity, even destructive of it. One of the hidden challenges is that even arguments that seem to advocate for practices that go beyond existing regulations still manage to import the notion of research undertaken on "human subjects"—a term that has its legacy in medical research (see, e.g., King *et al.* 1999).

Fundamental and concrete differences reside in doing ethical research in the social sciences as opposed to clinical or medical research. Sarah Maiter *et al.* (2008:308), relying on Susan Boser (2006), provide some useful general insights about research ethics in the fields of medicine versus the social sciences: the health and medical sciences have "typically not been attentive to social relationships 'inside' the research process," while most researchers in the social sciences have embraced the "'expert' perspective, adopting an objectivist stance that does not encourage introspection regarding social interdependencies among researchers and researched." Thankfully, these insights have become more commonly acknowledged over the past few decades. These differences point to the impossibility of firming up research in the social sciences with the ethics guidance provided by medically based codes. If the audit culture in universities works with a medically based framework of assessing research ethics, one can expect difficulties for the social sciences.

As Deborah van den Hoonaard and I wrote (D. and W. van den Hoonaard 2021), inductive research is one of the contested areas in research-ethics review, being the source of considerable friction. Within the framework of inductive research, the validity of good ethics is not based on the potential to make research findings generalizable from data. Inductive research leads us to the idea that knowledge is not "objective." In many respects, the researcher generates data and findings from personal interactions with the research participants. There are many angles to one's findings—all contingent on the place of the research participant, of the researchers, and of the types of issues being explored. The notion of working with hypotheses is out of tune with the inductive approach.

It is important to acknowledge the objectives of social research. For the purpose of analysis, social research regards individual human beings as the repository of social meanings. Even though social researchers engage in observing or interviewing individuals, they see them as the fulcrum of those social meanings. Researchers eschew personality traits, do not invent motives, and are more likely to answer the question of "how" rather than "why"; the former leads one to understand the social process, whereas the latter limits understanding to motives. As Deborah and I (D. and W. van den Hoonaard 2021) claim, social scientists are not experts in people's lives. A social perspective leads us to understand the broader structures that give rise to how people interact with each other and live out their lives.

In contrast, it is abundantly clear that medical and clinical research identifies separate individuals as the source of data. Worries about obtaining individual consent and about avoiding risk or harm derive from the primacy of the individual in one's research. However, the individual is not an autonomous being that exists in isolation from others, therefore it makes no sense for social researchers to view individuals as standing alone in their ideas and interactions with others. Individuals are social entities. Notions around anonymity, privacy, or confidentiality are extremely variable across cultures.

What stands out in qualitative research is its emergent design. Were such research to proceed according to some initial plan and without any change over the course of the work, colleagues would be suspicious. The unpredictable and emergent nature of qualitative research is one of its strengths. Along with field notes, the researcher's musings and reflections about the research and preliminary findings go a long way towards strengthening the research. The analysis of interviews must be accompanied by additional notes and insights typically gained during or after the interviews have taken place (see Box 4.2 of D. van den Hoonaard 2018).

One strategy in conducting ethical social research is to *decrease* the distance between the researcher and research participants. Social interactions that occur between research participants and the researcher are ongoing and always changing. Only by being closer to research participants can we more fully grasp that process. The wide range and variety of methods in field settings where social research is conducted are incompatible with the imposition of a single standard ethics code (D. and W. van den Hoonaard 2021).

Abbar Husain (2018) writes about a rich variety of methodological approaches, including the study of graffiti, cartoons, photo-elicitation, the contents of refrigerators, archives, neighbourhood walks, listening to street noise, and the analysis of social media data. It is not unusual to hear presentations at the annual Qualitative Analysis Conference[1] that cover seventeen research methods. Understandably, ethics committees may be bewildered by, or may have misgivings about, such a variety of methods. There is thus an "insufficient appreciation or understanding of how each study in the social sciences calls for a different ethical 'accent': anonymity might be an impossibility, confidentiality unnecessary, and consent an empirically troublesome issue with regard to employing methods that engage collectivities" (D. and W. van den Hoonaard 2021:247).

Since the mid-1990s, we have witnessed a growing trend among researchers to archive and share qualitative data (Feldman and Shaw 2018). Numerous scholars who are trying to respond to the idea of creating archives and sharing data seem to implicitly endorse the idea that qualitative researchers should, one way or the other, conform to the idea of data sets. However, some have raised concerns about "the assumption that qualitative data are similar to and can therefore be subject to the same treatment as quantitative data" (Parry and Mauthner 2004:140). This leads to problems because "data" in qualitative research consist of notes related to observations, interviews, and the like. The idea of data "sets" is therefore quite foreign.

There are other data protection systems, such as DA-RT—Data Access and Research Transparency—initiated by the American Political Science Association, but this has proved to be as unsuitable as other ethics-review systems. Understanding qualitative data involves a series of complicated interpretations, which then each only makes sense in the context of many other interpretations.

As with the use of a wide range of methods, it would be impossible to design one ethics code that could satisfy the diversity and multiplicity of research settings. The volume edited by Kleinknecht *et al.* (2018) demonstrates the variety of settings and populations that are involved in sociological research, including, for example, studies of the marginality of women and of others (Benbow and Hall 2018), truck drivers (Fleming 2018), organizational settings (Hillier and Milne 2018), transgenderism (Johnston 2018), military personnel (Wright 2018), pick-up artists and personal reputation (Kleinknecht 2018), the female escort industry (Wojciechowska 2018), action on streets (Landry 2018), children's sense of place (Akesson 2018), and the private space of the home (Mannay 2018). Each research setting involves its own relevant method: on-site observations, interviews, photo and textual analysis, online research, ethnography, and so on.

It is essential to recognize the role of the larger social and cultural contexts in the lives of research participants. Deborah van den Hoonaard (2005) finds that interaction and research are collective acts. Humans adjust to others or purposely resist that adjustment. Gary Alan Fine's description of the social context of workers in a kitchen (1996:222) illustrates this point very well: "The workplace—the kitchen—becomes a staging area in which meanings are generated, often through talk, but these meanings do not merely float in an undefined space but have effects on relationships and a pattern of action."

Researchers need to recognize and understand the larger social context in which individual lives are situated. Even if the research involves interviewing just one person, that person's life always implicates others. One cannot escape enmeshment in a web of interrelations. No research, if conduced ethically, can ignore that social reality. We can extend this critique to the dependence on automated transcription and analysis software.

We can ask: Which of the above elements are prescribed or described in the formal medical research-ethics codes, whether pertaining to the individual or the larger social and cultural contexts? None, as far as we know.

Long before the resentments and lack of enthusiasm among researchers in the social sciences became apparent, universities embraced the growing audit culture. Formally viewed as an opportunity to implement transparency, universities welcomed the accountability inherent in audit culture as an opportunity to engage in cost–benefit analysis of their administrative processes and products. One could also note that the basis of audit culture is grounded in assumptions of untrustworthiness. Ethics in research served, paradoxically, as a test of trustworthiness.

Audits have pervaded public and semi-public institutions, including universities. As a tool of management, audit culture has become robust and indispensable. It has become a permanent part of the institutional firmament. The audit "explosion" (Power 1999) is premised on the need to assimilate and make sense of the diverse constituent parts of the university. Thus, audit culture is averse or even allergic to diversity, and tends to collapse disciplines under the broad umbrella of interdisciplinarity. As such, any inherent understanding of sociology must be subsumed under a more broadly defined set of criteria. On the surface, the penchant towards interdisciplinarity appears to be a positive development—indeed, what could be more deserving of praise from the public and politicians than an approach that allegedly integrates all the sciences? However, John Holmwood (2010) writes that interdisciplinary codes of research ethics are not up to the task of meeting ethical standards specific to sociology or anthropology.

More seriously, one is inclined to believe Holmwood's (2010) claim that interdisciplinarity has subverted sociology as a discipline. With the growing desire in universities and other research funding venues to advocate interdisciplinarity, sociology has had difficulty maintaining not only the value of its own concepts and methodologies, but also its disciplinary identity. The rise of audit culture has further constrained the distinctiveness of sociology and has forced proponents to adopt less sociology-oriented approaches. As a consequence, any distinctive ethics claims within sociology have to be forfeited, and rearticulated and reformatted in a way that sustains the possibility of audits. Holmwood (2010:1) speaks of "an increasingly blurred distinction between sociology as a discipline and the interdisciplinary area of applied social studies."

Research-ethics review follows the university's preference for interdisciplinary research and, as a consequence, it uses the practices and habits of interdisciplinary research to orient itself. Self-captivated by the fever of interdisciplinarity, the methods and approaches specific to the social sciences are becoming muted. It is not a distant step of ethics committees to align themselves with the medical framework of research ethics—something that has already been formally recognized.

In the context of research-ethics review, audits have acquired the unassailable term of "governance." The use of this term makes it nearly impossible to challenge it, critique it, or revise it. It has become a bulwark against any attempts for change. It is not unusual for those who advocate contemporary ethics codes (such as Panigrahi *et al.* 2017:1), and who also wish to promote research integrity, to note the relevance of "good governance in research practices" to "avoid any misconduct." Many universities, like the University of Edinburgh, for example, aver that researchers are committed to maintaining the highest standards of research integrity in all aspects of research, ensuring that research is conducted according to appropriate ethical, legal, and professional frameworks, obligations, and standards (University of Edinburgh 2021). While lofty, this stance undermines the tenets of social research, trying to assimilate them to legal prescriptions and dismissing all research that is not considered "rigorous."

There are also voices at the other end of the spectrum who suggest that "despite these laudable intentions, there is a growing chorus of complaints within universities about these ethics committees and their proliferating regulatory regimes" (Kohn and Shore 2017:229). These authors point to the "spread of new managerial systems of accountability and risk management" (*i.e.*, the rise of audit culture within universities). Marilyn Strathern, drawing widely from the scholarly literature, offers the most compelling argument about the linkage between ethics review and audit culture. She reminds us that, "[a]ccountability practices have become a central part of the re-invention of government" where "audit and ethics are structuring social expectations in such a way as to create new principles of organization" (Strathern 2000:281). "It has become an emerging principle of social organization" such that "the language of ethics is proliferating" (Rose and Nilsson 1999:19). Patricia Lotich (2022:1) follows the public perception that "auditing is an independent, objective assurance and consulting activity designed to add value and improve an organization's operations." She claims that organizations have vowed to themselves (and others) that audits can exemplify "policies and procedures to maximize efficiency and create consistent practices," and that non-compliance becomes a serious matter and must be reported "for corrective action." Adherence to the belief in objectivity, cast in a legal framework, makes audits a troublesome part in the life of scholars who value relativity and are passionate about their interests in a given topic or approach. Under the cape of a single system of medical research-ethics codes, one can see how the approach taken by researchers in the social sciences can be easily (and legally) interpreted as an act of non-compliance.

Kohn and Shore (2017:229) aver that "social scientists, particularly those who do ethnographic fieldwork, find themselves increasingly at odds with the assumptions that underpin these committees' judgements about what constitutes research ethics or indeed what constitutes viable 'research.'" Taking this point further, Carl E. Schneider (2015) asserts that the current model is so fundamentally misconceived (and its implementation so often misguided) that efforts to foster ethical research conduct are actually undermined. According to Schneider, institutional bias in favour of the hard sciences and the biomedical model of research are the main reasons why applications from researchers in the social sciences are not successful.

The narrow mission of protecting research participants, as was the original mandate of research-ethics committees and especially of institutional review boards (IRBs) in the United States, has succumbed to a greater mission, namely to scrutinize research applications in ways that create barriers even for low-risk projects (Dougherty and Kramer 2005:183). Norwegian scholars Truls Juritzen, Harald Gromen, and Kristin Heggen (2011:641) pull no punches when they write that all ethics committees are fully implicated in exercising full power, and that these committees claim that researchers are "powerful, potentially uncontrolled and dangerous." Such a view, according to these authors, leads committees to wield power beyond their original intent. Similar views are advanced by Robert Dingwall *et al.* (2017:3), who remind us that "the systems of research governance... frequently reflect concerns with institutional legitimacy and the performance management of academics." Apparently, this audit system prevails because it prioritizes reputation above academic freedom and the protection of research participants. Adam Hedgecoe (2016), for example, shows how a research-ethics committee restricted research that could prove to be embarrassing for its university. The fact of universities' use of ethics committees for internal discipline is indisputable.

Recent neo-liberal debates about the value of the social sciences (as well as the humanities) are weakening the argument to have the system accommodate these fields, contributing to a loss of identity of specific disciplines. When interdisciplinary research aspects are applied, the aspects particular to sociology evaporate. Ted Palys and John Lowman (2010) identify as "vanilla" research that offends no one or research that does not challenge the *status quo* (see also Taylor *et al.* 2018). Marco Marzano, in "Sociology and the New Ethics Disorder" (Chapter Five of this volume) pursues the theme of so-called "vanilla" research in an urgent manner.

The next chapter turns to the key feature of my argument about research-ethics codes and research-ethics review, namely that the medical ethics framework has fully captured the research-ethics perspective of all disciplines. This capture has ravaged the social sciences.

# 3
## *The Capture* of the Social Sciences *by the Medical Ethics Framework*

RESEARCH-ETHICS COMMITTEES are the instruments that create disparities between the exigencies of the medical research-ethics framework and the unmet needs of research ethics in the social sciences. Researchers in the social sciences will inevitably fall off a moral cliff as a consequence of having to follow the inapplicable medical-ethics codes. All of this is due to the fact that the medical research-ethics paradigm holds a privileged position in the research-ethics world. The power of that position creates a wall of silence when critics propose alternative approaches in research ethics. However, there is now a growing awareness that the biomedical framework has captured Indigenous research ethics, for example. Given the new awareness of the needs of Indigenous researchers to establish their own frameworks, we can be thankful that the period of capture was very brief in this particular case.

The privileged position of the biomedical research-ethics regime has had a capturing effect that fosters disdain for alternative forms of doing things (see, *e.g.*, Giddens 1991); it maintains for itself the right to interpret the world as it sees fit, and, in this case, reshapes the world of ethics in research. When I first considered the impact of the biomedical research-ethics framework on the way social scientists had to regard ethical issues, I initially thought that the best way to describe that relationship was in terms of dictation by the biomedical framework. Given that in current literature the term "colonization" has increasingly become used by scholars to describe many social settings (such as in education), the use of this term forecloses its specific and more appropriate use to refer to indentured or dispossessed peoples, seized (Indigenous) lands, enslavement, displacement, or forced migration (Tuck and Yang 2012). The idea of "capture" therefore represents a more useful description of the social process I am trying to describe in this book.

However, drawing on the thoughts of Frantz Fanon (1963) in *The Wretched of the Earth*, there are nevertheless useful connotations from that earlier literature and its notions of colonization. For example, colonization proves to be very effective when the colonized themselves take on the perspective of the colonizer. It is not difficult to visualize how some social scientists in this connection have taken on the view that the biomedical research-ethics framework is something that is more useful to researchers in the social sciences than a framework originating in the social sciences. In his preface to Fanon's book, Jean-Paul Sartre shares his understanding of Fanon's perspective:

> In the colonies, the truth stood naked, but the citizens of the mother country preferred it with clothes on: the native had to love them, something in the way mothers are loved. The European elite undertook to manufacture a native elite. They picked out promising adolescents; they branded them, as with a red hot iron, with the principles of Western culture; they stuffed their mouths full with high-sounding phrases, grand glutinous words that stuck to the teeth. After a short stay in the mother country, they were sent home, whitewashed. These walking lies, had nothing left to say to their brothers. (preface to Fanon 1963:7)

They could only echo the truths they heard in a European motherland (*i.e.*, the biomedical research-ethics framework). Sartre, in that same preface, deduces from Fanon's writing that atrocities in the colonies seek "to dehumanize them [and that] everything will be done to wipe out their traditions, to substitute our language for theirs and to destroy their culture without giving them ours" (preface to Fanon 1963:15). Fanon speaks of "colonial estrangement" and that "decolonization, which sets out to change the order of the world, is, obviously, a program of complete disorder" (Fanon 1963:36). Along those lines we learn that, under colonialism, "the native is declared insensible to ethics; he represents not only the absence of values, but also the negation of values" (Fanon 1963:41). In the end, the biomedical ethics system forms a structure wherein all researchers must be imbued with the same approach to ethics. It is crucial to remember that researchers so captured by that system are not merely dominated; the crux is that the system inhabits the mind of those researchers.

These sentiments may sound far-fetched in the genteel world of academic ethics where raging inconsistencies among disciplines are muted. But in fact, they fact fall short of expressing the true reality of the brutal conditions caused by the capture of the research-ethics system by the medical model.

## What Is Behind the Face of Capture?

The ideas in this book are not born out of policy makers' lack of concern about doing ethical research, nor do they smack of medical researchers' desire to supplant ethics codes in other research domains. Rather, it is the privileged position of medical ethics codes that has led policy makers into believing that these codes are superior to those in other disciplines. Their temporary (we hope) success rests on their mandatory nature in the larger scheme of all research in the world. That nature has led researchers outside the medical realm to adopt them into their own schemes of how to do research ethically. The biomedical scheme of ethics has thus captured all other disciplines. It is by now a tiresome critique to point out that the prevailing medical research-ethics system lacks relevance to the social sciences. The first critiques of this system date back to 1977 (Wax 1977; Barnes 1977). It should therefore not come as a surprise to anyone that the medical ethics framework has created an ethics disorder for the social sciences. It is naive, however, to suggest that this disorder is solely the result of the capturing effect of regulations in medical ethics. The growth of audit culture in universities, as pointed out in the previous chapter, and of capital-intensive research with its penchant for deductive research are also, as I have already noted, responsible for this disorder. The surge of interdisciplinary research, too, has made sociological research less central in our ethical considerations of our own research. These forces, among others, have stymied the traditional methods of qualitative data analysis and the ongoing efflorescence of the social sciences. Faced with a remarkable slew of unethical research in the medical fields, government agencies busied themselves with fine-tuning the medical research-ethics regime. It was just a matter of time until the medical framework would embrace all research in all disciplines that involve the study of human populations. This capture removed all other research-ethics competitors from the field.

We researchers in the social sciences were asleep at the switch when the capture of the medical ethics framework began some 30 to 40 years ago. Universities and government agencies could not resist both the public prestige of the medical research-ethics framework and the corrective action needed to remedy its earlier medical research. Many researchers in the social sciences were up to their necks in their own work. They were too busy to take on the additional burden of resistance; the demands of their careers offered neither the time nor the energy to resist. Professional associations, too, were either unwilling or unable to take up the cause of arguing that the inherent medical model of ethics was inappropriate in the social sciences. There was, however, a rising awareness of difficulties. Zachary M. Schrag's analysis of the situation in *Ethical Imperialism* (2010b), as well as Laura M. Stark's *Behind Closed Doors* (2011) demonstrated the pitfalls of medical research-ethics codes for research in the social sciences. Ithiel de Sola Pool (1977), a pioneer in the development of social science and network theory, with a solid reputation as a leading authority on the social and political impact of communications technology, objected vigorously to this capture and was in fact one of the earliest scholars to organize a campaign among his academic colleagues. He recruited some 300 people for protests that involved an array of social scientists.

Like blowing leaves in anticipation of a storm, there were at first only a few scholarly articles that foreshadowed the impending threat to social research. Before 2000, there were merely a dozen articles. In 2002, a culture of fear became more apparent with the publication of no fewer than 50 scholarly articles, a number of book-length critiques (*e.g.*, Miller *et al.* 2002; van den Hoonaard 2002), and PhD theses on the topic (*e.g.*, Hamilton 2002). Today, we count more than 800 publications. Subscriber services such as ResearchGate and Academia often post announcements of new articles or books. Of the 80 posts I received between January 28, 2020 and April 13, 2020, 55 (69%) dealt with publications on ethics in research. Can one infer that there is ongoing interest in research ethics? Despite our concerns about the inadequacy of the biomedical model of research ethics and our noisy complaints about the profound lack of suitable terminologies (van den Hoonaard 2004b), qualitative researchers are not well placed to defend themselves (van den Hoonaard 2002). This dissonance has reinforced a "hurt perspective" whereby qualitative researchers now believe they are held more accountable than researchers with a positivist perspective (van den Hoonaard 2004a). Urban legends abound about the problems that researchers in the social sciences face in ethics committees.

Kerstin Roger and Javier Mignone (2018:49) report that ethics committees mounted obstacles to their research that, without their intervention, may have led to their studies not being conducted at all. In their experience, "ethics committees can follow a standard list of concerns they are tasked to raise, which may now, however, apply to participants in our research, or they may pose false barriers for inclusion in valuable research."

Like any situation inhabited by the pattern of capture, the ethics-review system conforms to a top-down model of research (Cross *et al.* 2015:1011) where researchers are "experts" and participants are "mere objects of study." As a result, we find ourselves in a state of surprise and confusion whenever medical research ethics indicate a need to include "justice" in its codes. For example, why are "subjects" not compensated for their participation in research, sharing in the profits of any successful marketing of a resulting drug?

Formal ethics codes leave no room for eventualities that can occur after the collection of data has taken place. The notion that one can predict in advance what kind of data will be of use leaves no room for the flexibility required of qualitative researchers, pitting the rigidity of REBs against the standards of the discipline. One researcher, I recall, was so distracted by editorial commitments on behalf of an academic journal that she lost her appetite to write up her data as originally planned. Ethics committees probably also offer a limited view of the outcomes of research: does formal public speaking about one's research qualify as an "outcome"? Can unreadable prose in a published article qualify as an "outcome"?

## The Nature and Functions of Research-Ethics Committees

Alison Taylor *et al.* (2018) question whether it is possible for a single bureaucratic policy to address a diversity of research-ethics concerns. In their experience, this goal is not achievable. Another enduring question about research-ethics review committees relates to their success in protecting research participants. Carl H. Coleman and Marie-Charlotte Bouësseau (2008) conclude that, despite the prominence of auditing procedures within the research environment, there is no empirical evidence that these procedures are effective at raising ethical standards. Further discussions in this volume will elucidate why it is so difficult to mount such an assessment. Outside of the medical ethics framework, there are very substantial differences of opinion (and fact) as to what constitutes the "protection" of research participants. Coleman and Bouësseau, for their part, are focused on health and medical research, pointing to significant global and regional health conferences that were launching pads to bring these concerns to the world stage. What is more, the studies that monitor the impact of ethics committees indicate more of "a culture of red tape rather than a culture of ethics" (Burris and Welsh 2007).

Researchers such as Jennifer L. Buckle *et al.* (2010:112) point to the proliferation of ethics committees concerned about research involving those who grieve. Their worries run completely counter to the typical experiences of bereaved research participants, who "frequently comment on the personal benefits they derived from the process of sharing their perspective in a detailed manner with an interested and engaged researcher."[1]

It has become a truism that researchers in the social sciences are dissatisfied with the current standards and procedures for assessing research ethics. These researchers well recognize the incompatibilities between the mandatory review process based on the medical framework and the research they do. They have noted that review committees require researchers to make early decisions regarding the formulation of the research question, the details of the design of the study, the consent process, and so on (von Unger *et al.* 2016). Ethnographic fieldwork and other approaches such as interviews—in fact, all inductive research—fall outside the conventional medical ballpark. Rena S. Lederman (2018:18) speaks of "design" versus "discovery" epistemologies—an apt description of the essential difference between deductive and inductive research. Every researcher in the social sciences faces the following dilemma: Do I go forward with the misshapen "corrections" based on what the review committee has in mind or do I withdraw my application from review? Given the amount of time, energy, and professional commitment the researcher has invested in a given study, the researcher must work "between the lines" or make do, knowing that some approaches cannot be undertaken (and will be buried in the act of the research itself), while at the same time trying to remain faithful to the style and methods of inductive research.

The English-speaking world has latched onto research-ethics review in a truly dedicated fashion; originally based on the ethical fault lines of medical research, the system has now expanded to cover all research that includes research participants in the United States, Canada, England, and elsewhere. When one talks about the kudzu invasion of American ethics into other nations, one does not mention the real driving force—American dollars, which are contingent on the recipient having a US-style ethics-review process in place. For the same reason, it is not quite accurate to say that the English-speaking world has "latched onto" ethics review; rather, ethics review was forced upon it. In Germany, according to von Unger et al. (2016), it was up to the various disciplines to draw up their ethics codes, although the influence of the Anglo-American world has no doubt started to exercise its influence over how research-ethics review can best be covered.[2] In 2008, for example, the United States Office for Human Research Protections (OHRP 2008) felt the need to compile a list of 900 laws, regulations, and guidelines in 84 countries, to assure that standards of human protection were followed. This 75-page document aims to instill internationally the concepts of research and human protection that are already standardized in the United States. The power of the medical research-ethics framework is clearly evident in a document that outlines research-ethics developments in Germany (German Data Forum 2016:2). This document defines some of the "key principles for research ethics" as constituting, "scientific integrity and the integrity of researchers," "avoiding harm," and ensuring "informed consent." Taylor et al. (2018:2), however, are hesitant to recommend the Anglo system to the wider world because "the current regime continues to emphasize the risks over benefits of research and its inherent conservatism discourages research aimed at progressive social change." These priorities will deter qualitative researchers from submitting their research plans for review. The German document (German Data Forum 2016) also advocates higher-level committees beyond local or regional ones, making it even more challenging for local qualitative researchers to have any say about the needs of their own research. This document is a checklist, with a brief explanation of each item. As a whole, it does represent a critical or analytical discussion of the research-ethics review process in Germany, indicating that the anglicization of research-ethics review is well under way. With regard to the scope of research-ethics review, one still finds policy makers and others speaking of "behavioural scientists" in reference to researchers in the social sciences. That term properly falls under psychology rather than sociology (Roth 2018).

While there are significant paradigmatic differences between the biomedical approaches represented in the current universe of research-ethics codes and the approaches used in the social sciences, it might be useful to underscore these differences in relation to certain key concepts that prevail in current ethics codes. Biomedical researchers take these concepts for granted; however, they take on a different value for social-science research. These concepts relate to *anonymity, confidentiality, informed consent,* and *vulnerability*. There is considerable depth of discussion attached to these concepts, but I confine myself here to a few examples.

With regard to *anonymity*, Katja Gunther (2009) challenges researchers to consider whether using pseudonyms is more relevant than using real names. It is the social context and the relationship with research participants that decides which use is more relevant. A study that aims to be transformative in line with the commitments of the participants calls for a more open process of naming participants. For example, Bonnie Scarth (2016) points to the ethical problem of using anonymity in some thanatology research, arguing that the decision of anonymity should at times rest in the hands of the participants themselves. Annukka Vainio (2012:686) is critical of using anonymity because of the unequal power relations in research that can prevail when anonymity is used. Avoiding anonymity can give power to the participants, allowing their words to be heard.

The 21st century brings on particular challenges related to digital media, specifically at the point of dissemination, which are only now surfacing (Tilley and Woodthorpe 2011). Difficulties can also emerge within the context of history and geography. Sources of funding, accountability to stakeholders, and involvement in knowledge transfer, among other factors, create pressures to rethink anonymity.

*Confidentiality* takes a particular turn when dealing with secrecy, power, and oppressive social structure. Benjamin Baez (2002:35) has long held the view that we need to "re-characterize" confidentiality in research away from "static notions of harm and privacy to one that accounts for a critical agency which exposes, subverts and redefines oppressive social structures." Research that takes issue with social injustice sees confidentiality as protecting secrecy, which "hinders transformative political action." How can one go about transforming society when "political action requires that researchers and respondents consider themselves involved in a process of exposing and resisting hegemonic power arrangements"? To the same end, Ted Palys and John Lowman (2010:265) lament how "excessive REB risk aversion" has forced researchers "to choose between exposing themselves to the prospect of going to jail to protect confidentiality, watering down their research objectives, or conducting 'vanilla' research rather than engaging in controversial and/or sensitive areas of study." There are more extensive discussions about the issue of confidentiality, but these few observations already permit us to see how research in the social sciences can be beset by concepts that researchers in the biomedical fields can simply take for granted.

The notion of *informed consent* is deeply shaped by cultural diversity (Barrett and Parker 2003), disciplinary conventions (Bell 2014), and fixed and fluid understandings (Bhattacharya 2007). The case of criminal populations (Coomber 2002) presents a genuine dilemma because the concept of free and informed consent is a strange artifact in prison research. Given that it is difficult to reconcile the consent process within numerous social and cultural contexts, and that it sometimes depends upon relationships with participants and the nature of the research discipline, the habit of securing consent could simply amount to "empty ethics" (Corrigan 2003:768).

While social scientists readily recognize the various forms that *vulnerability* can take, they are particularly apprehensive about the extent to which vulnerability can become a catch-all, imaginary concept. Cherry Russell (1999), for example, reports that researchers are likely to invent the motives or characteristics of research participants when they employ *a priori* ideas at the start of the research. Vulnerability, in particular, is a concept that seems to have distorted such research. My own research (van den Hoonaard 2018) has also dealt with this problem more recently. The moral cosmology of research-ethics review committees requires them to adhere to the basic values of medical research which, as I already have pointed out, stand far apart from the social sciences.[3] Ethics committees are, moreover, inconsistent in their approaches to evaluating social-science applications and ethnographic research (Castillo 2018). Initially, committees were likely to be headed by an experimental psychologist or a chemist who was seen to embody a clear and factual understanding of normal science. The style of communication varies depending on whether the researcher and ethics committee are located in a small or large university, highlighting issues of trust (van den Hoonaard 2011). Taylor *et al.* (2018:69) put it so well when they say that researchers must earn the trust of ethics committees but have to "demonstrate their compliance and willingness to do things in the standard way, while earning the trust of community participants often requires them to do things differently." As a result, "[r]esearchers have to become contortionists."[4] It also makes a big difference whether ethics committees operate within medical versus non-medical universities. Ethics committees can choose to ignore to particular issues, a phenomenon that Erving Goffman (1972:385) has called "civil inattention," and they may be subject to fads and fetishes in ethics review. Ethics committees may adopt literal or non-literal interpretations of ethics codes; for some, a formal or legalistic approach is the norm. While some believe that research using public documents is not subject to IRB approval, others believe that publication of professional conversations should now be determined by IRBs. In the experience of Debbie Dougherty and Michael Kramer (2005:185), the prospect of publishing conversations about experiences with IRBs was a "greater risk to human subjects...than in [publishing] them on other topics." The response of the IRB was "self protective, not human subject protective."

Dougherty and Kramer (2005) remind us of a number of ironies that attend to the decisions of the ethics committees. First, there is a move from protecting research participants to protecting the institution itself from liability. Second, because ethics committees feel entitled to approve research on professional opinions about those self-same ethics committees, they also shape professional conversations. Third, there is no oversight of the work of ethics committees. Fourth, ethics committees can claim access to consent letters from those who participated in providing comments to the authors who published a journal article about their views of ethics committees, making their participation risky—a contradiction of the purpose of ethics committees to protect research participants. As it turns out, the majority of the narratives documented by Dougherty and Kramer were critical of ethics committees. There are, moreover, inconsistencies in the adjudication of research proposals. Committees may hold undergraduate students to a higher standard than veteran researchers or not let the final reports of students piggy-back on earlier research, even though that research was supervised by a veteran professor (Taylor *et al.* 2018). The spirit of *Gemeinschaft* versus *Gesellschaft* has a relevant bearing on the nature of communication between researcher and ethics committee. What needs to transpire is the sense that both are party to a common culture of ethics, not just one determining the ethics on behalf of the researcher.

There are, moreover, pressures within ethics committees. The heavy workloads in those committees can prove to be a distraction. The attention to the details of the application forms potentially leaves little time to consider the larger ethical facets of applications (Truman 2003). The *modus operandi* of ethics committees revolves around the idea that it is better to be safe than sorry. Finally, communications between ethics committees and researchers are idiosyncratic and inconsistent.

Ethics codes do not spell out how committees and researchers should interact.[5] Ethics committees follow either very tight or very loose rules of engagement. The uneven dynamics of power between the ethics committee and the researcher remain a strong influence. The interactions between ethics committees and researchers devolve into cat-and-mouse games, with researchers hoping that this or that strategy may work. Researchers are timid about challenging the decisions of ethics committees. One cannot fail to note that men complain more often than women in this regard. A researcher is not likely to know what is meant by the notation "please explain" by a committee on an unsuccessful application. These vague comments arouse considerable anguish in the researcher because they do not know the ethics committee's assumptions behind such comments.

Both researchers and ethics committees either forgo or sacrifice ideas. Researchers resort to a *faux* magic, making up descriptions of their strategies just to satisfy REB requirements. Some researchers purposely avoid learning of the membership of ethics committee while others believe that obtaining details of the most successful applications will help them. Urban legends fill this space. Ethics committees are more lenient when researchers define their research as "preliminary," and researchers consider such tentative proposals as trial balloons. Strategies entertained by researchers include "Don't give ethics committees a cause to worry." It is also helpful to pitch the idea that one's research has "some risk" rather than suggesting it has "no risk."

Ethics committees tend to perceive potential dangers with almost all research and want to find ways to curtail those dangers. This perception leads researchers to describe research-ethics committees' approach as "risk-averse conservatism" (Taylor et al. 2018:69). Research-ethics committees use unusual methods to define populations as risky. Dougherty and Kramer (2005) found that when a person feels uncomfortable about an event that occurred long before the research has started, that person falls under the rubric of research-related risk. Committees regard some populations as needing enhanced protection from research; exceptions to his category include un-incarcerated white males aged 18–65 and white females after menopause, but before retirement. After retirement, one falls under the category of being vulnerable to research risk.

Qualitative researchers now have to resort to using positivist and medical research terms—the use of the dominant language as a performative strategy. Researchers navigating ethics committees and ethics codes face a task not unlike that of walking in an unfamiliar city without the benefit of a map, not knowing what unexpected dangers and obstacles lie ahead. Erving Goffman's concept of "secondary adjustment" (Goffman 1961:171) is relevant here. A secondary adjustment is "any habitual arrangement by which a member of an organization employs unauthorized means, or obtains unauthorized ends, or both, thus getting around the organization's assumptions as to what he should do and get and hence what he should be."

Many other practical considerations by ethics committees do not resonate with research in the social sciences. The start and end dates of research are social constructions that ethics committees inflexibly invoke, and factors such as minimal risk, length of interviews, and whether or not recorded data should be destroyed are subject to decisions that affect the approval process of projects. Ethics committees believe that confidentiality in focus groups is a potential problem, or that courts of law (in Canada) can force researchers to reveal the names of research participants, as was the case of research about a massive wind farm being built in Quebec (Kondro 2016).[6] Snowball sampling, a recruitment practice in which research participants assist researchers in identifying other potential subjects, allegedly poses dangers to maintaining anonymity. Committees may even see unsolicited data as problematic. Some committees dislike researchers' making preliminary contact with research participants. Howard S. Becker (2004:416) surmised that a researcher probably needed to avert her gaze when she came into contact with participants if "she had not been able to make the proper arrangements" with the research-ethics committee. Similarly, Ingeborg Helgeland (2005) discovered that her ethics committee did not want her to contact possible research participants in advance of her research, even to see if there would be any interest on their part in participating in the research. Taylor *et al.* (2018), experts in community-based research, point to the same problem with their own work as well as that of others. One also learns that ethics committees require social researchers to use medically defined disorders as opposed to what research participants and some researchers in medicine or psychology might claim as a self-diagnosed disorder. Researchers may be required to destroy data and even personal research diaries. Ethics committees inform researchers that they must opt for "higher" ethical standards, although the meaning of this phrase escapes the researchers. Cover letters for surveys or documents requesting consent have a legalese rather than an ethical or softer tone (Grayson and Myles 2005). The researcher is left to wonder what would constitute a "significant" change in the research if they are called upon to make such a change. To be sure, these formal and informal rules are the underlife of research ethics; they are found across all ethics committees, albeit unevenly and with variable seriousness.

## Immediate Consequences for Social Research

According to Julian Baggini (2018:7), social scientists who attempt to fit their ethical approach into the prevailing framework of medical ethics soon believe that they have "run off a moral cliff, impossibly suspended in mid-air," realizing "there's nothing under [their] feet." They must quickly satisfy the demands of the medical framework to save themselves from falling into the abyss. They must juggle unhelpful legalistic and social expectations. Rejecting the standard medical ethics framework, social scientists are regarded as ethics nihilists.

Other, more concrete, consequences of research-ethics review are immediate and drastic. Master's theses in sociology and anthropology have become homogenized with respect to topics, and they have become methodologically impoverished and less diverse in their range of approaches (van den Hoonaard and Connolly 2006).

Today's social researchers prefer the interview method over any other method. They now steer away from ethnography or participatory research. One researcher reported that a reviewer of the third edition of her textbook, *Qualitative Research in Action: A Canadian Primer*, suggested removing the chapter on observation as no longer relevant (D. van den Hoonaard, personal communication to W. van den Hoonaard, April 20, 2020). The interview nowadays resembles a deductive, experimental procedure. For many researchers (and ethics committees), questionnaires and interview "protocols" are *de rigueur*, even though these methods now stand kilometres apart from the nature and purpose of in-depth and inductive interviews. It is evident that the choice of topics has become impoverished, which, in turn, has led to a lack of diversity and richness of research in the social sciences. As the influence of the bioethics framework expands its regime around the world, social-science researchers are finding smaller niches within which to conduct research according to their own sociology and interests. The transformation of the social sciences has been unparalleled. Of the 200 scholarly books I explored during 2002–2004, only 27 have incorporated research participants (van den Hoonaard 2006a). A so-called ethnography now contains only interviews. Ethics applications avoid mentioning valid research approaches such as "hanging out," field research, research-journal entries, or natural-disaster research, as these methods face unpredictable outcomes in ethics committees. Moreover, ethics committees have not grasped the detailed analytical work surrounding the interview. The teaching of research through in-class projects has in some cases become prohibited, even for research covering mundane topics. Certain critical topics are harder to research because of the difficulty of obtaining consent early in the process. Lynne Roberts and David Indermaur (2003:289) speak of the challenges involved when prisoners are required to sign consent forms because these forms are a record of voluntary participation in a research project, "providing the potential for research documentation to be subpoenaed and posing a threat to the prisoners' future." Sociological research that questions authority is usually off the table. These cumulative effects lead one to consider the moral cosmology of research-ethics review committees that deeply affect (or infect) relations with social researchers. This cosmology underscores the primary ideological differences between official codes based on medical research and the prevailing ideas of ethics in the social sciences. We end up "othering" ourselves and exhibiting a false disciplinary consciousness (van den Hoonaard 2013b).

# 4 The Anthropological Stance *in Ethical Research*

**IN ALL RESPECTS,** the ethics maze in anthropology is a labyrinth unlike in any other discipline.[1] The relatively long history of this discipline means that it has had to face its ghosts of the past. Anthropology's empirical forerunners have taken part in missionary activities, embraced colonization, promoted the exotification of other cultures, and implicated governmental bureaucracies. In contemporary times, anthropologists have come face to face with the moral complexity of their research and with the pitfalls of careerism. In the first instance, they must ask themselves where their loyalties rest: Do they rest with the people they study or with their discipline? In the second instance, should they ponder whether careerism leads them to take shortcuts in their research settings, when their work would normally require them to spend a generous amount of time in the field? With respect to these considerations, ghosts of the past always seem to lurk behind the scenes, ready to reveal themselves unexpectedly as moral dilemmas.

Unlike sociology's striving to formulate a contemporary ethics code, anthropology's efforts mostly pertain to the broader relations and outreach activities of that discipline, whether these affect close relationships in the field, with informants, government agencies, students, sponsors, or the public. Although the discipline has its roots in the professional exotification of cultures and peoples, anthropology currently maintains a deeply felt recognition that peoples everywhere should hold the right to advance their own knowledge and contributions.

Exotification and respect for people's own values represent two opposing perspectives that have been woven into the tapestry of anthropology's past. At first glance, anthropologists exemplify a rather wide circle of topical interests when it comes to ethics. *EthNav* (2018), an online guide that enables researchers to orient themselves in an "increasingly congested landscape of expectations and regulations," offers critical insights about (a) why anthropologists often experience difficulties when it comes to research-ethics regulation and governance; (b) the sorts of ethical challenges social anthropologists face in practice; (c) how professional codes relate to the undertaken research; (d) examples of different approaches to ethical governance that are available online; (e) what ethics review is and how we arrived at where we are; (f) what the relationship is between sponsors of research and its ethical conduct; and (g) how we can distinguish morals from ethics, and what constitutes virtue in the context of anthropological research. Although these varying rubrics create worries, they still offer clear and refreshing insights about doing ethical anthropological research.

One is inclined to reconceptualize anthropology's involvement with ethics as a *grand plan*. It does not represent a fascination with the precarious details of *consent, anonymity,* or *confidentiality*. Rather, anthropology's primary and broader contribution lies in its efforts to respond to a modern-day quackery of "nationalism and racial snobbery" (Benedict 1934:10). It is an answer to the failure to understand "the relativity of cultural habits," which has barred citizens "from much profit and enjoyment in our human relations with peoples of different standards, and [made us] untrustworthy in our dealings with them" (Benedict 1934:11). At its basis, anthropology advocates a cultural and civilizational humility, and frowns on any attempts to prefer one's own culture in a world of many cultures. This stance greatly resembles that of humanitarian associations opting for the greater good (Pels 2018a).

With regard to the origins and development of ethical approaches, it is striking to note that what shaped the ethical paradigm(s) in anthropology was its orientation to historical and cultural issues outside the discipline itself. In each instance, these orientations caused major and radical shifts within the discipline. What is more, the abundance of topics and fields within anthropology prevented the ossification of the discipline, opening it up to endless rounds of debates about ethics. At least sixteen fields fall under anthropology, including ethnology, archaeology, political anthropology, biological anthropology, museum anthropology, evolutionary anthropology, cultural anthropology, economic anthropology, linguistic anthropology, medical anthropology, psychological anthropology, anthropology of food and nutrition, anthropology of religion, anthropology of work, urban anthropology, and visual anthropology. The scholarly and professional association of anthropologists, the American Anthropological Association (AAA), also represents professional associations attached to each of these fields. Anthropology constitutes a historical jumble of aims and practices.

Those aims and practices produced two distinctive aspects in the field. Marie Louise Pratt, among others, avers that one finds two genres, namely the "manners and customs" genre and the "academic ethnography" genre (1985:119). These genres are not as disparate as they seem. Peter Pels and Oscar Salemink suggest that the driving force of the "manners and customs" genre lies in the far-reaching interest in travel diaries cultivated in one of Europe's pre-modern eras. We learn from Pels and Salemink (1994:22) that this genre was "integrated in the tourist gaze." Following Toby Volkman (1990:91), this gaze is a distinctive gaze that can also become a "model for local gazes." Volkman, however, concludes that anthropologists have not quite decided what to do with tourism because it can be a blight on the local culture, and intrudes upon and threatens the "privileged domain" of anthropologists.

The other genre, "academic ethnography," incorporated ethnographic descriptions into a wider circle of theory. It is not difficult to see how colonialism entered the doors of both genres. The former feasted on a desire for exoticism, while the latter entered the fray of what would interest missionaries and colonial rulers, such as a preoccupation with the inculcation of beliefs that would support colonial rule. While travel diaries were relegated to the level of personal observations highlighting events or ceremonies that captured the attention of observers and writers, academic anthropology rose to occupy a "scientific" understanding of tribes, groups, and populations, which many thought would add to our common stock of knowledge. The ethical premises of both genres, however, did not differ widely. How would ethics play into our collective fascinations with "exotic" cultures? How would colonialism enter the ethical fray? In either case, power differentials would lead the ethics debate. At its best, academic anthropology could "also play a role in the resistance of minorities to state power" (Pels and Salemink 1994:24).

The resistance to state power became evident as early as 1919, when, according to Peter Pels, anthropologists "claimed professional ethical independence from colonial administrators, missionaries, or traders when… Franz Boas denounced anthropologists acting as spies for the American government" (Pels 2018a:392). With the rising political power of the United States during and after World War II, the ethical stance in anthropology shifted more concretely, resulting in the creation of an ethics code in 1971. Ruth Benedict wrote *The Chrysanthemum and the Sword: Patterns of Japanese Culture* (1946). at the behest of the United States Office of War Information in order to better understand and predict the behaviour of Japanese people during World War II. In that light, it is no surprise to learn that anthropologists would later study counter-insurgency movements in Latin America in the 1960s (Biswas 2015).

The contradictions inherent in such power dynamics were so enduring that they reflected a "tension between an Occidental discourse on ethical duplicity and a more specifically anthropological epistemology of double identities" (Pels 1999:101). This moral duality implies "an unintentional use of 'double standards' in professional practice." As explained below, one might well speak of a moral triple identity—that is, a *tri*plicity, not merely a duality. After all, anthropologists obtain an identity not only in relation to their sponsors or funders, but also in relation to their careers and to their participants in the field.

After World War II, anthropologists committed themselves to peer review and to the sanctions of a professional association directly borrowed from doctors and lawyers (Pels 2018a). The codification of ethics based on a professional model came late to anthropology, namely in 1948 (Israel 2015). The editors of *Human Organization,* the premiere journal of the Society of Applied Anthropology, were soon led to comment that the issue of ethics still seemed to trouble some of their colleagues (Society of Applied Anthropology 1951). Some of the leading ethical preoccupations involved the manipulation of research by its industrial and political sponsors, but also by anthropologists who accepted industrial support and compromised the research as a result. In this connection, the (applied) anthropologist is required to point out measures to be taken in the case of a crisis or disturbance, when asked by a special interest group to undertake research with the aim of changing an organization to be studied.

Not to make the moral dilemmas any easier, anthropology contains a wide variety of fields of study, from physical anthropology to ecological anthropology, to name two. But it is in the parallel field of applied anthropology where the ethical concerns of anthropology have required researchers to learn through experience. Applied anthropology is not a field that can be remotely conducted from an armchair or computer screen. It is a field where ethics has pushed itself to the forefront of all concerns because of its multilayered and multivaried connections across a broad spectrum of audiences. The field must hold a deep and simultaneous concern for: private sponsors of anthropological research; government agencies; the commercial exploitation of traditional knowledge of Indigenous people; the role of permissions of Chiefs or Elders for conducting research; cultural differences as they affect gender, age, and education; the wide range of interactants in the research setting; the sway of public opinion; and even for contrasting philosophies and approaches within the discipline—all in the face of, or despite, political or military colonization. A later section in this chapter discusses how anthropologists wear three hats.

In May of 1946, applied anthropologists were the first to consider a code of professional ethics (Mead *et al.* 1949). The Society of Applied Anthropology thus became the scientific organization in the area of social and psychological sciences that concerned itself with developing a code. Their report asserted that the goal of applied anthropologists was to see the "greater well-being of the individual through change" (Society for Applied Anthropology 1951:4). Two years later, members of these disciplines revised and circulated a statement, adopting it after two and a half years. Apparently, the report relied heavily on the Committee on Ethics of the International Preparatory Commission for the International Congress on Mental Health held in England in 1948 (we note the explicit medical framework of this report). Issues that came to the fore in those days included: the relevance of an anthropologist's behaviour as a private citizen and as a scientist in peace and war; the unavoidable influence of hierarchical and bureaucratic structures; collaborations involving colleagues and informants; public relations; and government (Mead *et al.* 1949). The 1948 Code of Ethics was drafted in response to American anthropologists' connection to the internment of ethnic Japanese residents by the United States during World War II. That code decreed that *no* anthropologist would "undertake a commission on behalf of any interest, or segment or section of a group..." (Society for Applied Anthropology 1951:4). The evolution of anthropological research-ethics accompanied these widely changing perspectives about the discipline itself.

Pels (2018a:392) notes that a "1949 American attempt [to codify research ethics] foundered and it was only during the Vietnam War that the momentum to draw up an ethical code gained sufficient force to produce the AAA's *Principles of Professional Responsibility* of 1971." Interestingly, the "first article defined the interests of the people studied as paramount and came down heavily on secret and clandestine research." A few years earlier, in 1967, the AAA had issued its first statement on ethics. Citing other research, Biswas (2015:251) stated that anthropology's bad reputation would close off future opportunities abroad, and that anthropologists feared that anthropological data would either "control, enslave, or even annihilate many of the 'third world' communities."

The revisiting of ethics issues in 1971 by the AAA seems to echo a process that started in the 1920s, according to Caroline Dillman (1977). The year 1925 represents the dividing line in anthropology as it moved from fieldwork *observation* to *participation* in the field. That change became a crucial element in the way anthropology began to see its ethical requirements. Advocating for the powerless (Adams 1981:155) became the one "pervasive, overriding obligation." Even classical works in anthropology—whether Colin Turnbull's *The Mountain People* (1987), Arthur J. Vidich and Joseph Bensman's *Small Town in Mass Society* (1958), or John Lofland and Robert Lejeune's "Initial Interaction of Newcomers in Alcoholics Anonymous" (1960)—"became the subject of gang attacks" (Dillman 1977:405) for their invasion of privacy and disregard for exposing the lives of individuals and communities.

By the 1970s, anthropologists became painfully aware of the political and moral implications of power. "Tribal and peasant minorities," we learn from Anton Blok (1973:95), were being "ruthlessly incorporated into larger political frameworks." This experience led anthropologists to see the need for an "enforceable ethical code regarding the relations between anthropologists and the people they study" (Blok 1973:95). A number of anthropologists suggested that scholars should either refrain from publishing the results of their research or withdraw from an area altogether. Blok (1973), however, believed that neither of these steps would solve the ethical dilemmas. What was needed was better and more information on those who control minorities in ruthless ways. From this premise follows the recognition of an obligation to the well-being of peoples being studied. Relatedly, researchers should "refrain from accepting funds or employment from a sponsor who would prohibit uncensored publications and interpretation of findings" (Jansen II 1973:326). This approach carries several other implications, namely that anthropologists work only for organizations whose goals they can agree with, not work for a government's department of defense, and that no secret or clandestine research ought to be done. The lack of strict boundaries in research, it is believed, may prevent opening up new areas of research and "yet untouched realms of data" (Jansen II 1973:327).

In 1973, marking 22 years in matters of ethics in anthropology, the concerns of the AAA underwent a major new shift in its deliberations, producing a new statement.[2] Responsibility towards research participants became the first concern. This approach included the need to inform participants of the impact of the research on their welfare. Anthropologists were now to give their sponsors "the best of their professional knowledge" (Jansen II 1973:326), while at the same time refusing to enlist sponsors who would censor publications. Loyalty also became an issue: one owed loyalty to the discipline and the sponsor. While the anthropologists should not become involved in doing research for the United States Department of Defense, they still should be responsible to both home and host government. Truth and candour would be the hallmarks of research (Jansen II 1973).

Pels did not think it a surprise when, "in the early 1980s, American academic anthropologists were first outnumbered by those in extra-academic employment; anthropologists working outside the academy wondered how they could countenance an ethics that elevated the interests of people studied over their employers" (Pels 2018a:392). The 1998 version of the AAA's statement asserted that "researchers must be open about the purpose(s), potential impacts, and source(s) of support" (Biswas 2015:251). Social anthropologists in the United Kingdom and in the Australia voiced the same sentiments in 1999 and 2003 respectively. Anthropologists in India created their own ethical space in 1970 to cast off a colonial legacy and to foster a preference for action research and demographic research, among others. After all, the rise of physical, molecular, and anthropomorphic anthropology had already become a growing phenomenon. It is also true that, unlike in the medical or health sciences, Indian anthropology has given less importance to the dominant bioethical issues of the Western world. The reasons may be manifold. Practicing bioethics in the Indian field context is challenging. The high number of non-literate individuals and the presence of external pressures such as social/political/religious influences make it difficult to introduce a project before studying the participants and to obtain informed consent.

Other issues are somewhat complex in nature. More broadly, anthropologists criticize some components of bioethics because of its abstract principles, which are derived from armchair philosophizing and reflect an ethnocentric view and a ready-made ethical code of conduct that lacks cross-cultural analysis. Biswas (2015:252) opined that "[c]ultural relativism recommends not to prejudge the ways of behaviour which describe a society." It should also be noted that ethics may differ significantly from culture to culture, or even within a culture.

A renewed interest in ethics, reflecting the current experiences of anthropologists, has pushed many of them to see ethics in research as an individual matter. As noted earlier, anthropology has had ongoing contact with a plethora of agencies, organizations, peoples, associations, and societies. These connections lead to various exigencies for characterizing specific ethics prescriptions. No single AAA code of ethics could possibly meet the diverse needs of anthropologists. An approach that empowers the individual anthropologist to make ethical decisions therefore seems to be the most useful one. Ethics rules, in this context, may pose dangerous limitations. The scope of anthropology should not be narrowed by the will of an AAA committee. In any event, it is impossible to do research without invading people's privacy (Jansen II 1973).

In summary, the history of anthropological research provides a glimpse into how complex the evolution of ethics within a discipline can be. Anthropology has several forerunners; the discipline covers many subfields and there is a variety of venues where field research is conducted. Moreover, it must satisfy many audiences, including sponsors, readers, and research participants in a wide variety of settings. All of these elements generate ethical dilemmas; some dilemmas evaporated as the nature and purpose of anthropology changed while others still lurk as ghosts. What is more, the distinction between anthropologists inside academic settings and those outside of those settings has had a significant bearing on how ethics policies took shape. Anthropology also faces new dilemmas.

Contrary to the detailed attention that ethics policies in general give to consent, confidentiality, and privacy, anthropologists have busied themselves with the larger, more encompassing ethical elements of their discipline. In the end, it has meant that the discipline has cultivated a wariness of governmental influence or interference, has become more entrenched in showing respect for the culture of research participants, has heightened the role of the individual anthropologist as the carrier of moral values (as opposed to adhering to formal codes), and has become more mindful of ethical requirements and of the moral and political implications of power.

The ethical reflections of anthropologists have also led to the realization that when conducting research, researchers must assume three identities, which in turn shape their ethical proclivities: an identity that arises out of their attachments to the funders of the research, an identity that reflects the relationships that develop during fieldwork, and an identity that comes with their own personal attachment to their career.

This chapter has also noted that the rise of research-ethics review is altering the research approaches in anthropology. In short, interviews are increasingly replacing ethnographic fieldwork. Throughout it all, the gravitational pull of the medical research-ethics framework is still in place and is, in fact, becoming stronger.

Marco Marzano

# 5   Sociology

## and the New Ethics Disorder

THE ADVENT OF ethics regulation (Haggerty 2004; Schrag 2010b; van den Hoonaard 2011), the dissemination of the informed consent myth (Marzano 2012), and the strict surveillance activities of ethics committees, first in the United States and then, progressively, throughout the world (Israel 2017), have had extremely serious consequences for sociology, particularly for qualitative sociology (van den Hoonaard 2002; Hammersley and Traianou 2012). Qualitative research, more than any other sociological approach, centres around the building of intense human relationships with the people studied.

Before setting out these consequences in detail, I would like to specify that neither in sociology nor in other social sciences (such as anthropology) was ethics regulation in any way bound up with any harm social research may have had on those involved in sociological research. In countering this truth, the exponents of ethics regulation never fail to single out, from among the thousands of social research projects conducted prior to 1980, the case of Laud Humphreys's (1970) empirical work, which generated the book *Tearoom Trade*. As is well known, Humphreys observed and then described—without revealing that he was a researcher and was adopting a voyeuristic stance—clandestine sexual encounters between men in the public park toilets of a large

North American city. He went to the extent of recording the license plates of those involved and then later tracking them down and interviewing them (obviously without mentioning that he had first observed them in this "prohibited" context).

Even in this case, the research seems not to have harmed those unwittingly involved (Yanow and Schwartz-Shea 2018). Quite the opposite. The effect of *Tearoom Trade* was to signal in a dramatic way the existence of a considerable number of people obliged by the homophobic narrow-mindedness of the American society of the day to confine their sexuality to a clandestine sphere. Humphreys himself became a militant defender of gay rights (Galliher *et al.* 2006), and refused to hand over to the police his research data (containing detailed information on those who took part in these sexual encounters), stoically accepting imprisonment and restrictions on his freedoms as a result (Mitchell 1993).

Thus, to no real benefit—because there were no real costs requiring a remedy—the advent of the era of ethics regulation inflicted serious and considerable harm on the qualitative research of sociologists who immersed themselves professionally in the everyday lives of groups, communities, or organizations.

Some of this harm extends to ethnographers as a whole. For example, consider the fact that qualitative social research projects are largely designed after fieldwork is already under way. Because ethics committees have to decide in advance the presumed harms involved in research, they hold the power to block research and to shape the forms and methods to be used in future interactions in the field. This is certainly a serious handicap for qualitative researchers. An equally serious risk is that the actions of these committees go beyond ethics and make their presence felt in the epistemological, methodological, and political choices made by scholars. Thus, such actions seriously limit researchers' freedom and their right to adopt non-mainstream approaches that are generally less well received by ethics censors (van den Hoonaard 2002; 2011; Hammersley and Traianou 2012).

# Cooperative Approaches
# and Regulatory Ethics

It should be noted that the impact of ethics regulation is not uniform across the board in qualitative research. Many scholars who make use of cooperative approaches of anthropological origin (Douglas 1976; Christians 2000), akin to anthropologists who study non-Western societies, whether currently or in the past, primarily study small individual communities or a vulnerable, marginalized group labouring under some form of social stigma. There are still others who believe that the purpose of the social sciences is to give a voice to those generally without a voice. They seek the assistance of those they study, taking care, above all, to gain an empathic understanding of their culture and improve their standards of life. The advent of ethics committees and the obligation to obtain informed consent create serious obstacles to the development of a natural friendship and goodwill with those taking part in research. A relationship of trust, empathy, and cooperation is required for a beneficial research outcome and the "conversion" of the ethnographer to the cause of the studied group (Davis 1973). This approach, according to some scholars, might develop more effectively from fieldwork carried out in complete freedom than from the application of rigid protocols in which the relationship between scholar and research participant(s) is to be paralleled with a seller–client or bureaucrat–service user relationship (Boser 2007). In such cases, the divergence between the culture of ethics regulation and that of researchers is all about means and not about ends. That researchers must be 100% honest, transparent in their intentions, and loyal to those studied is never contested. What the advocates of the cooperative approach argue is that all these objectives can best be achieved in a natural way, through researcher–participant relationships based on mutual knowledge, empathy, and friendship. They see bureaucratic formality, or worse, police-type surveillance enacted by ethics committees as useless and damaging forms of interference. These interferences are also harmful because they bring in an element of distance and aloofness to the spontaneous warmth that characterizes the close relationship between the researcher and the research participant(s). A clear example of the convergence between the ends of the regulatory culture and more cooperative approaches is embodied by the fact that cooperative researchers avoid revealing the unpleasant aspects of the lives of those they study and, if they do so, feel at fault, seeing themselves as having violated an implicit agreement and done unnecessary harm to the subjects of their research (Ellis 2007). Ultimately, Everett C. Hughes (1971:436, cited by Douglas 1976:43) well describes the philosophy of the cooperative approach: "the sociological investigator cracks the silence, but buries the secrets, one by one, in a tomb of silence—as do all the professions which deal with the problems of people."

## Ethics Regulation and Radical Humanism

There is a component of the community of qualitative sociology, however small today, that has suffered much more than others from ethics regulation, namely that current of thought that Richard G. Mitchell (1993) called "radical humanism." It is profoundly bound up with European sociology and philosophy and, more specifically, with conflict theory (Collins 1975; 1988) and hence with Marx's work and Marxist tradition as well as that of Weber (with the exception of Parsons's optimistic, functionalist reading; see Clegg et al. 2006), Simmel, and their respective contemporary followers (for an original symbolic-interactionist reading, see Athens 2017). Casting farther back in time, the mandatory reference representing this perspective is the naturalrealist philosopher Thomas Hobbes.

From this perspective, secrets (Simmel 1906; Goffman,1959), lies, and half-truths (Zerubavel 2006) are not exceptional, rare behaviours but a normal part of our social lives. They are the prerogative of all social classes and groups, observable at all geographical latitudes and in all cultures (Mitchell 1993), and they relate to the various spheres of social life, not only those associated with sex and money. In this approach, the suspicion that we are victims of lies, deceit, and scams is so ubiquitous across all societies that we humans react by adopting strategies in our everyday lives to ascertain whether those we come into contact with are lying to us. For all intents and purposes, we define these tools as "investigative" (Douglas 1976). As attested by David Shulman (1994), this term captures the inclination and ability to inquire into the sincerity of those we meet. Withholding or misrepresenting the truth frequently takes complex and organized forms (Costas and Grey 2014): firms misrepresent the quality of their products in advertising, churches conceal the existence of sexual abuse within, restaurants cover up the way food is made, doctors (even in contexts requiring informed consent) hide the full truth from their patients of their state of health. Lying is systematic and multi-level in politics, in corporate life, in hospitals, barracks, and many other aspects of common life (Bok 1999). The motives that lead people to play with the truth are manifold; people lie, for example, to keep hold of or win power, safeguard their reputations, obtain some financial benefit, and much else besides. Humans certainly do cooperate, but they do so within a limited circle of contexts and behaviours. Conflict is at least as normal as cooperation in social life. In this context, rigorously obeying the dictates of the regulatory culture espoused by ethics committees and revealing one's research intentions to the subjects of research with total and unconditional honesty effectively means giving up studying much of the social context of research participants, including all that is tied to aspects of their lives that they prefer not to reveal.

We do not, in any case, need to share the radical humanist vision of society to acknowledge that many forms of covert research are indispensable and irreplaceable if the functioning of everyday life in complex societies is to be understood. In fact, not only does an awareness that humans are being observed and studied frequently induce people to behave in unnatural, artificial, and misleading ways, but research subjects are often not even aware of many things relating to them that are of interest to researchers (Johnson 1975; Douglas 1976).

Researchers are thus obliged to resort to some form of deceit or subterfuge if they are to achieve their research goals. Overall, whatever the preferred theoretical approach, the illustrious examples of covert research in sociology's history are many. I will cite just a few of the most famous and rightly acclaimed here (for a synthetic description of the contents of the research cited, see Calvey 2017).

I refer to Paul Cressey's (1932) pioneering (and completely undercover) research on so-called taxi dance halls in 1920s Chicago and the many subterfuges adopted by researchers during the Hawthorne Studies, that great research program led by Elton Mayo (1933) in the 1920s and 1930s, which led directly to the creation of the Human Relations School. Or think of Howard S. Becker's (1951) ultra-well-known research on North American jazz musicians. As Becker himself recalled years later in *Outsiders* (1963): "Most of the people I observed did not know that I was making a study of musicians. I seldom did any formal interviewing but concentrated rather on listening to and recording the ordinary kinds of conversation that occurred among musicians" (1963:84). Industrial and organizational sociology would have missed out on a great classic if Donald Roy's (1952; 1959) New York garment factory research had been blocked. For this research, Roy had himself hired as a drill operator in a machine shop for a year without revealing his identity to anyone. If Roy succeeded in casting light upon the social and human dynamics of working-class labour, Melville Dalton (1959) managed to describe the complex warp and woof of the social and professional lives of managers in what may have been the longest and most challenging covert research project in sociological history. It uncovered the existence of an underground corporate life made up of cliques, clans, and networks of various sorts. It is to Jack Douglas and his assistants (Douglas *et al.* 1977) that we owe a meticulous description of the sexual encounters observed on the La Jolla nudist beach in San Diego. Finally, in this systematic gallery of examples, I would like to cite what is probably the most universally known work, namely Erving Goffman's extraordinary *Asylums* (1961), the result of a semi-covert research project in a New York psychiatric hospital in which only the staff knew what this great sociologist's objectives were.

# Qualitative Sociology in the Censorship Era

What have been the consequences in the wake of the advent of ethics regulation and the resulting banning of covert research? I have identified three, all of which are negative.

## 1. Diminishing the public relevance of sociology

Obeying the dictates of ethics regulation and avoiding all forms of covert research have led to a powerful reduction in the contribution of qualitative sociology to the public debate (Burawoy 2005). What can be concluded, from observing sociological work as a whole, is that where qualitative researchers submit (as they are now obliged to almost everywhere in the world) to regulations articulated by ethics committees, they end up researching only politically innocuous subjects and people whom researchers consider friends or towards whom they have positive feelings. A single example will suffice, involving the disturbing phenomenon of trade in human organs. University of California Berkeley researcher Nancy Scheper-Hughes (2004) was required to apply for a complex exemption from the ethics rules that normally applied to anthropologists in her department. If this exemption had not been granted, she would have had to go with pen and informed-consent forms in hand to the human-organ traffickers who were the subjects of her inquiry!

Radical humanism and realism have effectively been pushed to the margins, and the critical social-conscience task of empirically illustrating many of the more delicate mechanisms of social-system functioning has been entirely delegated to investigative journalism—a field that has been strengthened and consolidated during the same years in which qualitative sociology has declined. Think of the spectacular success achieved by undercover journalistic investigations, for example, by Günter Wallraff (1985) into Turkish temporary migrant workers in Germany, by Barbara Ehrenreich (2010) into low-income workers in the United States, and by Roberto Saviano (2007) into organized crime in Naples. These and many other undercover investigations (such as the extraordinary Watergate investigation) were carried out without any official authorization. In the belief that damaging the powerful when they behave badly is not morally inappropriate, but is in fact morally right, many of the journalists responsible for these inquiries have marshalled what have always been the best qualitative research tools: narrative, vivid description, and impassioned storytelling (Langlois 2011). Ultimately, as Joan E. Sieber and Martin Tolich (2013) have argued (see also Matheson 2018), journalists have always had the right to freedom of speech as an absolute precedent in moral terms, in contrast with the current situation for researchers, for whom the rules imposed by ethics committees are prioritized above freedom in research and writing.

The impact upon world public opinion of the investigative journalism cited above has been similar to that of certain great undercover academic research studies of the past: would the anti-psychiatric movement have been capable, in certain countries (including in my own country of Italy), of achieving the closure of asylums without the contribution of research like Erving Goffman's (1961) or David Rosenhan's (1973) in the field of social psychology? How much poorer would research into the psychological and social bases of Nazi authoritarianism have been without Stanley Milgram's (1974) experiments? How much longer would Americans have had to wait for LGBTQ rights without research like Laud Humphreys's (1970) work, with its ability to illustrate the existence of an underground, long-suffering gay world? And the list could go on.

The fact is that qualitative sociologists have made a significant contribution to public thinking and political debate in ways that investigative journalists are continuing to make today. The difference is that social research has contributed to the public debate not simply, as journalism inherently does, by describing what is happening in certain worlds, but also by interpreting and explaining such phenomena, fitting them into a comparative framework, and making ongoing attempts to conceptualize. At least in principle, academic research should be freer than investigative journalism (Galliher 1980), given that academics do not work for organizations owned by wealthy magnates, financiers, or billionaire industrialists, and this should make them better placed to reveal important truths about power and the powerful. The old adage of "speaking truth to power" is very relevant in sociological research.

## 2. *Exalting an individualistic vision of social life*

The culture of ethics regulation places the protection of the individual interests and rights of research subjects at centre stage. The obsessive individualism that permeates ethics-regulation practices derives from an ultra-liberal political vision as well as from the undisputed hegemony of medical culture in the research world, resulting in the researcher–participant relationship being put on a par with the doctor–patient relationship. In the social sciences, however, this is an entirely misleading parallel. Unlike the researcher–participant relationship, the doctor–patient relationship is always cognitively asymmetrical because doctors always have a monopoly over the truth related to what is happening to patients' bodies (unless the patient is a colleague). Medical knowledge is completely inaccessible to patients in the vast majority of cases. Even the immense quantity of information made available on the internet cannot level the playing field or fill the knowledge gap between doctors and patients. Doctors understand what is happening to a patient's body and decide whether or not to tell the latter, whatever the latter's social or economic status or power. Doctors with good communication skills have the capacity to deceive their patients with varying degrees of ease, even the rich and powerful, such as to encourage participation in experimental research.

The relationship between social researchers and those studied is very different from this doctor–patient relationship. To a considerable extent, it is the research participant who knows his or her personal truths and decides whether to sideline the researcher or agree to be observed and respond honestly to questions. It is the research participant and not the researcher who "owns" the truth. Researchers can potentially use the truth they learn maliciously, misrepresenting and distorting it, but subjects can also lie to researchers, manipulating the truth and thus giving half-truths or a false description of their activities. Ethics regulations run the risk of inadvertently facilitating this possibility, by depriving researchers of the social investigation tool of undercover research.

Given this, I would like to argue that researchers certainly have a duty to respect all human beings *as such and in the same way* but they *do not have a similar duty to treat all the social roles, organizations, and institutions in their studies equally.* The formal equality preached in research-ethics codes risks legitimizing an overall power imbalance, thereby benefiting the rich and powerful and effectively negating the significance of one of the most profound and authentic structural aspects of all societies: social stratification, namely the presence of class, income, status, race, language, and other differences. For sociologists, this element should be unacceptable. By definition, sociological research deals not with individuals but with groups, organizations, and social roles. It is clear that all these social structures have been created and peopled by individuals, but over time they take on a life of their own—which cannot easily be changed by a single individual. The following is an example: when sociologists study the actions of the board of directors of a large corporation, they are in no way interested in the personalities or personal profiles of its individual members. Rather, their focus is on the way the board makes environmental decisions, its relationship with politicians, its safeguarding of collective interests, its vision of the future, and so on.

From this perspective, incidentally, the practice (in ethnographical accounts) of preserving the anonymity of research participants serves not only to safeguard their privacy and right not to be recognized, but also to focus attention on their roles rather than their personalities, on what they do rather than who they are. In contrast to what is generally the case in investigative journalism, the purpose of social research is not to report specific cases of moral deviance, malfeasance, or corruption but rather to illustrate the structural and organizational mechanisms that ultimately generate moral deviance, malfeasance, and corruption, among other things.

If this is the case, then it is truly difficult to argue that there are not enormous discrepancies between groups and organizations in terms of their power and social reputations, and that these do not imply significant differences in research methodology. Certain groups, organizations, and social roles are immensely more powerful than others, and thus are more capable of safeguarding their own considerable interests, blocking researchers' access to the information they seek, and protecting themselves (including legally) from the consequences of the publication of research results relating to them. It is thus inevitable that researchers who want to discover something truly significant about the most powerful organizations—to lay bare their secrets—must be able to work undercover. In such cases, power asymmetries work in ways that are precisely the opposite of the default assumptions of ethics committees, who assume power is in the hands of researchers. In fact, the power dynamics work entirely to the benefit of the organization being observed: on one side there is an ethnographer armed solely with notebook, audio recorder, and plenty of enthusiasm; on the other side there is a powerful organization with millions of dollars, retaining hundreds or thousands of loyal employees (who may even collude in covering up terrible secrets), housed in buildings that are physically impenetrable to outsiders, with a legal department capable of destroying the reputations and lives of anyone daring to tell truths that the organization prefers not to confess.

By not taking account of such elements, ethics committees end up considering all groups and organizations in the same way, and, as a result, they make it virtually impossible to study the more powerful organizations; individual researchers are thus encouraged to choose weaker and more marginalized groups as the objects of their studies. Gathering data on these groups and organizations is more straightforward and requires less work. Furthermore, members of weaker groups are frequently anxious to obtain social legitimacy and improve their reputations, including by means of the results of social research, and they are also less aware of the potentially negative consequences for them of published research. In response to these issues, some scholars (*e.g.*, Barnes 1976) suggest that research with marginalized groups should be accompanied by certain sanctions, in order to avoid inadvertently cultivating prejudice.

The point is, however, that continuing in this way risks our knowing everything about the behaviour of the less powerful, who have few secrets, and nothing about the powerful, who have a great many skeletons in the closet. This is certainly not a result to be proud of.

### 3. Implicitly giving up the right to free speech

In giving up investigative methods, sociologists risk abdicating what, for Michel Foucault, is human beings' most moral activity: that of exerting parrhesia, that is, telling the truth to those who are afraid of hearing it or who do not want it to be told. As Gary Alan Fine argued (2019:839), ultimately "it is our task to describe the world as it occurs, not out of malice, but as our responsibility." To affirm an uncomfortable, unpleasant, and embarrassing truth, above all before the powerful, and at the risk of paying an extremely high price, has the same meaning for sociologists as it does for other people: it is to take the most courageous and virtuous path imaginable. For this and for all the other reasons set out in this chapter, I believe that researchers who have told some small, innocent lies for the sake of the truth—that is, who have engaged in minor deception in order to be able get at a truth that they then make public—can be fully forgiven. It is an action that realist Niccolò Machiavelli would have approved of. As Anna Traianou quite rightly said,

> [c]ontrary to what is sometimes assumed, Machiavelli did not propose that rulers and other political agents should pursue evil ends. Rather, he argued that they will often have to use means that are regarded as morally questionable, such as deception, and even sometimes those that are abhorrent, such as war, *in order to pursue effectively ends that are good*. (Traianou 2018:171)

The need to use morally questionable methods emerges from the realist affirmations that (a) social life is complex; (b) human beings are not easy to know; and (c) humans are animated not only by altruism, goodness, transparency, and a desire to cooperate with others, but also by other less honourable or positive sentiments. For sociologists doing investigative research, this means, in Weberian terms (Traianou 2018), choosing responsible ethics over ultimate ends and being willing to accept all the consequences of so doing.

## 6   Current Debates in the Research-Ethics Community

**IT SHOULD COME AS NO SURPRISE** that current debates among social scientists represent a panorama of views aimed at resolving the dilemmas posed by research-ethics review codes, processes, and deliberations. Eight different sets of proposals fit within four broad categories, with many proposals having soft boundaries. Ideas migrate conceptually from one set of proposals to another. Migrations also occur over time when one set of ideas seems to be more feasible than another set, when some scholarly explorations seem to hold greater promise than others, or when individual scholars become less certain about their original propositions. It is not easy to fit these ideas into distinctive slots. By narrowly highlighting each of the eight sets of proposals, one cannot make room for how ideas travel back and forth across the borders—hence the need for discussing the proposals in terms of broader categories.

The first—and least flexible—category consists of a distinctive approach to tighten current research-ethics codes. The second category seems to have gained the widest support among critics of research-ethics review. This category encapsulates the hope to make the system itself more amenable for researchers in the social sciences. Specific proposals involve rebalancing the current ethics-review system, either by changing the deliberative and consultative process of ethics committees, limiting the scope of these committees, or taking into account the social context of ethics review. Proposals in this vein do not change the current structure, but favour in-house adjustments that represent manageable reforms. A third category requires a more fundamental structural change across the entire span of ethics review. Its advocates argue for a regulatory split between medical research and research in the social sciences. The other option in that category suggests that policy makers implement a new structure, fresh from the ground up. A fourth category is bolder in its outlook. It demands that policy makers eliminate all regulations. In that same breath, there are a few scholars who advocate the adoption of a research covenant—it is a proposal that I stand for and something that will be discussed in this book's final chapter.

It is of interest to identify the disciplinary sources of all these proposals. Are researchers in medicine and psychology, for example, more attracted to conservative approaches (*i.e.*, rebalancing the current research-ethics review structure) because they are already committed to the founding principles of the structure? What are the disciplines of those who favour an entire reconfiguration of the regulatory ethics-review structure? Finally, what is the disciplinary backdrop of scholars who favour doing away with the whole structure?

In our despair about the dilemmas facing research-ethics review, one might be inclined to offer broad and bland solutions—cries from the wild, so to speak, in the form of poorly thought-out approaches. The most productive approach is not obvious: Do we just pull away from the medical framework and repudiate, item by item, that which does not sit well with us? Does self-regulation offer a way out of the dilemma? Do we put something in place that is based entirely on the actual research activities of social scientists (von Unger *et al.* 2016)? Or do we go into the specific details of the medical research-ethics framework that irritate us? Along the way, some of us might list the following as undesirable outcomes of this framework: using signed consent forms (Roberts and Indermaur 2003), avoiding sensitive research topics, inventing vulnerability (Lee and Renzetti 1990), exaggerating harm (Inckle 2015), limiting research on marginalized groups (Helgeland 2005; Cloke *et al.* 2000), favouring anonymity (Tilley and Woodthorpe 2011), or avoiding engaging in participatory action research (Boser 2007). We need a complete overview of the perspectives that many scholars and researchers offer as a remedy to the dilemma of research-ethics review in the social sciences.

Meanwhile, I continue to affirm the idea of "ethics drift," a situation in which the horizons of research-ethics review keep expanding and where researchers, unfamiliar with these new horizons, keep bumping up against inappropriate rulings they are subsequently reluctant to appeal (van den Hoonaard 2004a). Moreover, very different ideologies may undergird the decisions of different ethics committees. Remarkably, there are also many different understandings as to what constitutes a "human subject" (van den Hoonaard 2003). All these difficulties inject despair and conflict into the process of research-ethics review. Nor should we ignore how the tension between ethical realism and ethical formalism creates divergent views with regard to the concepts of consent, confidentiality, anonymity, perceptions of harm, and human dignity (van den Hoonaard 2002). And what are we to make of the general lack of interest in ethics education (van den Hoonaard 2003)? Is the narrative of research ethics review driven by cautionary tales from past medical experiments? Regarding the dangers attached to ethnographic research, are they alleged or real (van den Hoonaard 2003)? Do the homogenization and impoverishment of social-science research constitute ongoing sources of worry (van den Hoonaard and Connolly 2006)? What accounts for the disappearance of critical research (van den Hoonaard 2004a)? How do fads in research-ethics review (van den Hoonaard 2006a) result in the kinds of proposals that are submitted? One is already aware of the problems of research-ethics review *vis-à-vis* qualitative research (van den Hoonaard 2002a; 2005).

These questions or issues feature prominently in some of the proposals for reform. In our search for a suitable proposal, we must unwittingly guard against adopting the terms and terminologies that reside in the medically based research-ethics framework. A side effect of this strategy means that we must try to avoid using the standard expressions found in medical research-ethics codes, lest we inadvertently fall into the embrace of medical research-ethics. After all, my burgeoning interest in seeking change in research-ethics review derives its basis from principles found in the social sciences.

We owe a debt to the many scholars and policy makers who have actively sought a solution to the dilemmas at hand. As mentioned earlier, current discussion about changing the research-ethics review process reveals a tableau of eight sets of proposals. These can be narrowed down into a schema of four broad categories. A brief overview of the proposals shows that social scientists lean towards views that are more "liberating" than the vast majority of researchers who work in law, biotechnology, psychology, education, social work, epidemiology, and medicine. There are a few exceptions, but the overall grouping of disciplines falls according to what one might expect in terms of support for each of the four categories below.

# 1. Tightening the Current Ethics Code

The proportion of those who advocate for tightening ethics codes is very small. Iain Brassington (2016), a philosopher, admits that the system may be flawed, but believes that dismantling it is not the answer. Brassington reminds us that the research-ethics review system is in place because of an accumulation of historic problems. Even beyond Nazi medical experiments, the Tuskegee syphilis study, and so on, there are still experiments that warrant ethical oversight. Kerry Breen (2002), a gastroenterologist, is a heartfelt supporter of the research-ethics system. According to the assertions of Susan Dodds (2002), Dean of Arts and Social Sciences at the University of New South Wales (Australia), it is difficult and still too early to assess the full impact of the Australian 1999 *National Statement on Ethical Conduct in Research Involving Humans* or to call for a major review of the ethics committee process. It would thus be premature to embark on any major overhaul of ethics codes. Yes, some ethics committees are overstretched, but the system is not on the verge of collapse. However, psychologist Sean Jennings (2012), while defending the role of research-ethics committees, also proposes steps for their improvement in the United Kingdom. He argues that the existence of ethics committees is justified by virtue of their role in improving ethical practice and in minimizing harms to research participants. He proposes a model of review that would best achieve these goals.

In this difficult period of debate about the regulation of ethics, we must understand that the strict application of ethics codes is now part of the neo-liberal marketization of higher education. The codes prioritize the individual, define who is the expert (*i.e.*, the researcher), and do not necessarily question the *status quo*. At times, too, we question whether ethics codes serve to heighten a sense of morality or whether they concern themselves with protecting the liability of universities.

## 2. Rebalancing the Ethics-Review Process from Within

The second category of proposals places constraints on current ethics regimes, whether it is by confining change to the work of ethics committees themselves, by changing the deliberations within committees, by recognizing the social context of social research, or by affording exemptions to particular research activities. This category has gained the widest support among critics of research-ethics review. My discussion of this set of proposals seems, in hindsight, rather long, but this category is an anvil upon which many remedies rest. It encapsulates a hope to make the system itself more amenable for researchers in the social sciences. The desire to rebalance the ethics-review process was triggered by a panoply of issues, some of them raised by qualitative researchers themselves. There was a push to demythologize the ethics-review process and to make the membership and the decision-making processes of ethics committees more transparent.

A significant issue is that the possibility of risk should not be exaggerated and regulations should be less harsh. Following an idea proposed by Rik Scarce (1994; 1995), there is ongoing interest in the idea of a "scholar's shield law," which would protect researchers from being compelled to testify against research participants and would ensure that research notes or transcripts involving research participants could not be subpoenaed. Kevin Haggerty believes that a Quebec decision on this matter has in fact made this a legal reality through case law (Kevin Haggerty, personal communication to W. van den Hoonaard, December 24, 2022).

Proposals in this category do not transform the current ethics-review structure but favour in-house adjustments that are manageable and do not involve substantial reform. The envisioned changes include limiting the scope of what should be reviewed, rethinking the nature and purpose of informed consent, and realizing that research—especially ethnography—has flexible start and completion dates.

To change the deliberative process of ethics committees is a challenge. The purpose is to liberate the consultative processes within ethics committees so that research proposals in the social sciences will be freed of the rigid attention paid to the biomedical framework of research ethics. Ethics committees will need to acknowledge the disciplinary diversity of research approaches and methodologies. This is easier said than done. Members of ethics committees are far too numerous and too invested in the medical research frame to commit themselves to changing their habits. However minute or large the changes envisioned, the proponents all agree that the research-ethics review system is here to stay, at least for some time (e.g., Haggerty 2022). Kevin Haggerty, by the way, is an advocate of the idea that ethics committees should publicize their decisions as well as offer a rationale for them. That is one step that could make transparent a review process that is often opaque, and it would inform committees about how other cases have been handled elsewhere. He also recommends that an ethics approval granted at one university should be accepted elsewhere at other universities. Accepting this suggestion would prevent frustration, exasperation, and loss of time and energy. Maureen Fitzgerald and Elisa Yule (2004:47), anthropologist and occupational therapist respectively, refer to the benefits of having "open committees," as opposed to "closed committees." In "open" meetings, discussions and decisions are open to inspection from the outside. Such meetings are advocated in the belief that "it can make the whole process more honest, transparent, and accountable—more ethical." As such it can improve relationships between all leading to better and "more ethically sound research reviews and projects."

Raymond De Vries, Debra A. DeBruin, and Andrew Goodgame (De Vries *et al.* 2004) explore three different aspects of research-ethics committees: (a) the composition of review boards; (b) the guidelines used by these boards to review research—and in particular, behavioural and health research; and (c) the actual deliberations of ethics committees. Some, like J. Michael Oakes (2002), a professor in social epidemiology, believe that researchers in the social sciences have the obligation to accept the legitimacy of research-ethics review; learn more about ethics-committee regulations, their imperatives, and the new pressures on them; and educate ethics committees about social-scientific methodologies and empirically demonstrable risks.

It is not only researchers who bear the onus of improving research-ethics review (by educating ethics committees about research, for example). The onus also falls on ethics committees themselves. Nancy Shore (2006), a social-work scholar and senior consultant for community–campus partnerships, interviewed ten community-based participatory researchers. Interviewees identified ethical issues relevant to their research, interpreted and reflected upon the Belmont principles, a set of ethical principles and US federal regulation generated by the *Belmont Report*, which provide the framework by which institutional review boards (IRBs) evaluate research. Differences were found between the researchers' views and the *Belmont Report*'s one-sided conceptualizations of these ethical principles. Shore's suggestions address these differences with the aim of strengthening the relevance of the process of ethics committees.

Jay Marlowe, who teaches counselling, and Martin Tolich, a sociologist, examine the significant gap that exists between the role of providing ethical guidance and that of providing support for community-based research (Marlowe and Tolich 2015). According to the New Zealand Ministry of Health (2012), "ethics committees in New Zealand serve as 'gatekeepers' that consider the ethical implications of a research." A relatively new group, the New Zealand

Ethics Committee (NZEC), formed in 2012, responded to the uneven landscape of access for community-based research. By offering ethical approval inclusive of the review of a project's study design outside of institutional settings, the NZEC has endeavoured to move beyond a gatekeeping research-governance function to that of bridge building. Marlowe and Tolich's paper reports on the NZEC's experience of working with community researchers to ascertain the possibilities and tensions of shifting ethics-review processes from research governance to a focus on research ethics in community-based participatory research.

Richard A. Shweder, anthropologist, and Richard E. Nisbett, social psychologist, underscore the opportunity to overhaul American policy and suggest limiting the scope of IRBs or their management by exempting low-risk research from the board's review. In particular, they advocate overhauling policy such that certain exempted research activities be excused from board review, and that there be no requirement that the IRB approve the exemption (Shweder and Nisbett 2017). Many other scholars, such as Benjamin Berkman *et al.* (2017), who work in the fields of bioethics or clinical research, are taking up these ideas with regard to even the very modest changes in what is known as "the Common Rule" (Dobrin and Lederman 2011) in the United States.

The most vocal proponents of changing the process of research-ethics review come from the ranks of qualitative researchers whose epistemologies stand in sharp contrast to those practiced in medical and clinical research. Gaile S. Cannella (2004), in the field of education, has come to believe that qualitative researchers who are informed critical activists regarding research ethics and regulation are urgently needed as voices advocating for appropriate practices that would protect all those involved—namely subjects/participants, researchers, volunteer academic reviewers, individual informants, the general public—while at the same time facilitating respect for research diversity. Economists Deborah Posel and Fiona C. Ross (2014) speak of an inevitable heterogeneity in research methodologies, field sites, and research relationships that make it impossible to have a one-size-fits-all system of ethical regulation.

One can classify all of the proposals in this category as bridge-building processes. They do not do away with the entire system of research-ethics review or create a parallel system for the social sciences alongside the biomedical paradigm. These scholars believe in the need to maintain a familiar system that would continue to create public confidence and a sense of trustworthiness (one should point out, however, that the public is probably not aware that such a system actually exists). The imagined notion of harm to research participants constitutes a major impetus to change the approaches of ethics committees, primarily by toning down notions of harm and rigour that would potentially work against applications from researchers in the social sciences.

Some speak of this approach as "situated ethics"—a system of ethics that brings the knowledge and decisions of ethics committees more in line with the research settings in which social scientists work. This approach mirrors the call to focus on a "localized or situated ethic" (Perez 2017). Todd Zywicki (2007) proposes reforms that would improve the research-ethics bureaucracy by narrowing its scope and increasing its efficiency. Although he refers to institutional review boards in the United States, his observations have broad relevance for research-ethics committees around the world. Judith B. Gordon *et al.* (2011) follow a similar line of thinking when they argue that it is possible for committees to improve the design of research protocols, provided that they become more aware of and responsive to the social contexts of all the actors involved in the research.

Valuable insights come from Teresa S. Perez (2017) as a result of her fieldwork in Cape Town (South Africa), which involved participant observation and covert research. Her ethnographic study enabled her to minimize the inequality between researcher and research participants. She wore a hidden recorder and obtained selective consent, which, she argued, was more appropriate than relying solely on fieldnote journals and signatures on consent forms. She concluded that a contextualized approach to ethical procedures was better suited to sensitive research topics, especially in research with marginalized social groups, where there is often a great deal of inequality between researchers and research participants.

Tim Bond (2012:111) believes that when ethics committees exaggerate the idea of harm, this ultimately causes damage to any realistic assessments of risk or harm. Such exaggerations, Bond suggests, "[add] persuasive power and authority to the speaker...by giving them a moral authority that trumps any more equivocal views based on the low probability of actual harm." Several other proposals emphasize the need for researchers to develop virtues and suggest making some of the requirements less stringent. A situated ethics such as this takes into account the particular and distinctive aspects of either the research setting or the methodology used to study that setting. Scott Burris and Jen Welsh (2007:643) write that "the emphasis by regulators on procedure is frustrating to IRBs and investigators and also contributes to an atmosphere in which review of research becomes an exercise in avoiding sanctions and liability rather than in maintaining appropriate ethical standards and protecting human participants."

Among the first stream of suggestions, Scott Burris (2008) acknowledges there is a poor fit between ethics committees and their assigned tasks. Some proposals—for example, those that call for setting standards, monitoring compliance, and disciplining violators—seem taxing for all. On the other hand, researchers in the social sciences should welcome the idea of narrowing the range of risks that the ethics-review process is expected to control. Burris incorporates ideas from other scholars who want to see internal reform, such as allowing for "routine prior review and be[ing] more modest (and hard-nosed) about the harms the system is going to try to prevent, and the investment appropriate to various kinds or degrees of harm" (Burris 2008:15). In these proposals, one senses a shift from relying on a regulatory scheme to a framework that emphasizes virtue. Michael Power (1999:17), for example, emphasizes virtue as "deeply bound up with a fear that the researcher is more or less blinded by self-interest." Similarly, John Cutcliffe and Paul Ramcharan (2002) indicate the need for an ethics-as-process approach. They focus on details about how interviews should be handled. However, their suggestion that informed consent needs to be scrutinized tells us that their proposal may not be entirely applicable to social scientists.

Lisa A. Eckenwiler *et al.* (2008) would like to see a more nuanced approach to bioethics. The goals of this paper—whose lead author holds appointments in a department of philosophy and a department of health administration and policy—were to encourage the World Medical Association to craft a declaration that (a) conceptualizes issues of vulnerability in richer and more nuanced ways; (b) resists the influence of profit motives; and (c) extends the scope of responsibility for ethical research more broadly.

Limiting the scope of research-ethics committees represents the second stream in this category of proposals, which addresses the imbalance between what the (medical) ethics codes demand and what researchers in the social sciences are seeking. One of the most prominent scholars in the field of research ethics, anthropologist Rena S. Lederman (2007), has placed many conventional topics in research ethics under the microscope and found them either wanting or irrelevant to the social sciences. For example, the notion of informed consent entirely misses the point in ethnography. She also queries: What is "research" in the first place? When does it begin and end? What is the relationship between its demarcations as a regulatory object and its demarcations in the everyday practices of knowledge production? Federal research-ethics regulations take for granted that research can be distinguished from non-research and subjected to distinctive constraints, but the regulations presume an idealized scientific method with predetermined spaces, times, personnel, and procedures. Several of these presumptions are inapplicable to ethnographic fieldwork. Lederman has performed critical work by analyzing the evolution of "the Common Rule" in the United States regulatory system (Lederman, 2011:83).[1] Lise Dobrin and Rena Lederman (2016) emphasize that regulation should specifically mention anthropology's core scholarly methodology, namely participant observation, and they offer arguments that participant observation should be exempted or even excluded from revised regulations. In their commentary on proposed changes to US regulatory system, they point out "that the ethical conduct of anthropological research requires sensitivity to context, which runs counter to the proposed rule's insistence on adherence to a common set of privacy safeguards irrespective of the situation (including the wishes of the participants)" (American Anthropological Association, 2016). In other words, their proposals would allow greater flexibility in obtaining and documenting informed consent.

The third and final stream that hopes to rebalance the perspective and decisions of ethics committees relates to the need to recognize the social context of research. Those who support this idea refer to it as "the new ethics." There is a greater recognition of the emergence of this new ethical framework (following Hammersley and Traianou 2012), particularly in cases where conventional ethical practices are supplemented by ethical practices that are designed to promote social justice. Herb Childress (2006) follows the same train of thought. He is a researcher, teacher, and administrator specializing in curricular design and outcomes assessment. He sees his work as an attempt to help young people view themselves as powerful actors in the world, and he aims to help them understand the ethical considerations this ability entails. In this light, he believes that "because ethics committee members are overworked, undervalued and given a thorny job, steps need to be taken to create a more collegial and collaborative arrangement, and one in which ethics committee service is enjoyable" (Childress 2006:85). A possible role of the ethics committee would be one of vision keeper and consultant; it might include a "board of elders" who help an institution and its members move towards socially positive research design, conduct, and outcomes (Childress 2006:86). This, of course, would require that researchers play a reciprocal role in which they seek to improve research practices in consultation with the ethics committee and provide the board with case studies of their own methodological leanings. This recasting of the ethics committee as vision keeper and consultant would imply a different sequence and style of interaction with researchers. Its first role would take place long before initial research proposals, through outreach to departments and graduate programs; this would place the "elders" in a position to guide community deliberations on research goals and social benefits.

    The European Commission hopes to find a way to match the kinds of ethical-practice requirements that are sought by biomedical sciences with all the non-medical sciences. This objective is interesting, but can these other disciplines all be treated as the having the same issues to address? How can divergences be managed and dealt with?

    The Council of the European Union (2015:3) asserts that "the primary responsibility for research integrity is with researchers themselves, with an overarching responsibility also being existent at institutional level." It "calls for the fostering of an institutional culture of research integrity in order to create, mainly through clear institutional rules, procedures and guidelines as well as training and mentoring based on the exchange of best practices, a climate in which responsible behaviour is expected at individual and institutional level." However, one wonders whether this particular approach goes far enough to remedy the shortcomings in ethics committees with regard to the social sciences and qualitative research in particular.

## 3. Introducing a Regulatory Split Among Disciplines

A third category of proposals aimed at solving the discrepancies between the medical ethics framework and the needs of researchers in the social sciences involves rearranging the regulatory structure itself—in other words, creating a regulatory split among disciplines.

Out of a desire to move beyond the adversarial relationships that have come to characterize the discourse between the upholders of the medically based research-ethics codes and those who see no relevance of those codes for their own research, there are those who advocate maintaining the institutionalized ethics codes for medical research, but insist that researchers in the social sciences use their own well-established disciplinary codes for conducting ethical research. Once we have moved away from this adversarial relationship, researchers in the social sciences will have no need to "other" themselves in research-ethics review; they can now own their own ethics in research (van den Hoonaard 2013b).

According to Scott Burris (2008), it is time to build two separate regulatory approaches—one for biomedical experimentation and another for social, behavioural, and epidemiological research (see also Bosk and De Vries 2004). In addition, Burris holds the view that we need two separate regulatory logics. One includes rules on conflict of interest, informed consent, and reporting adverse events. The other promotes a culture of ethics. It is time to rethink the role of ethics committees argues Dale Carpenter (2007), an

American legal commentator and professor of law. For decades, he notes, researchers have been coping with an ever-more intrusive bureaucracy that does not uphold basic academic values. Three things seem very clear: (a) the number of ethics committees has grown—to at least 4,000 worldwide; (b) these committees have recently "increased their scrutiny of social science protocols and all indications suggest even more scrutiny is imminent"; and (c) researchers in the social sciences are "increasingly frustrated, annoyed, and upset by decisions [of ethics committees], inconsistencies, delays, and misunderstandings" (Carpenter 2007:688). Carpenter suggests a different and more liberalized path. His platform of reform deals with the membership and structure of ethics committees, requiring basic First Amendment training for members. He would also require that the members have the expertise and competence needed to ascertain both the risks and benefits of the specific research they are reviewing. More significant, in his opinion, is that separate boards should be established at every institution for biomedical and social-science research. Carpenter holds the view that oral history and other interview-based research should be exempt from ethics approval, and that ethics committees reviewing research in the social sciences should be allowed to prohibit or alter the research only when the risks significantly outweigh the expected benefits. Moreover, a more radical proposal, in my estimation, involves ethics committees' reviewing or altering research and enforcing internal discipline on researchers, if necessary, "only after ethical breaches cause some harm" (Carpenter 2007:689). Carpenter claims that researchers in the social sciences, rather than ethics committees, should have the power to decide, in threshold cases, whether their research is exempt from prior ethics approval. Institutional liability should also be put on the table of possible reforms (and as a lawyer, Carpenter proposes detailed procedures to prosecute institutional liability.) He also offers the view that ethics committees can cause harm by being too risk-averse.[2]

It is clear that the proposed solution is American in character, without its being useful in the rest of the world. The American centralized, top-down approach is not a practice that can be easily transferred to other cultures and societies. C. Kristina Gunsalus *et al.* (2007) suggest that much of the stress in the ethics-review system has been caused by mission creep, with the result that the workloads of ethics committees have expanded to the point where they can no longer handle them effectively. As a consequence, these committees focus more on procedures and documentation, exaggerated precautions, and efforts to protect against lawsuits than they do upon grappling with difficult ethical questions. Significantly, these authors call for "refinements to our regulatory system that will provide a set of regulations designed for non-biomedical research." (Gunsalus *et al.* 2007:617). This approach allows IRBs to pay attention to areas where there is the greatest risk and to scale back in those areas that Carpenter (2007) has identified as presenting less risk.

Jocelyn Downie (2006), a Canadian research professor of law and medicine, argues that radical reform is urgently needed; she proposes the creation of a national agency in her country that would be charged with the oversight of research involving humans. The proposed agency would have three branches (policy and standards, education, and compliance). Each branch would consist of a number of independent national and regional research-ethics boards that no longer reside within institutions. There would also be an audit committee and a non-compliance committee (with a supporting staff of auditors and compliance officers). One might be inclined to interpret this suggestion as a means of making research-ethics review stricter.

In the United States, C. Kristina Gunsalus (2003), who heads a national organization for promoting professional and research ethics, asserts that because the current research-ethics review paradigm is heavily shaped by the medical paradigm, it is not a good fit for much scholarly work in the humanities, and evidence is emerging that the mismatch of regulation to these activities is causing projects to be delayed, abandoned, or never undertaken because of the effects of well-meaning but probably misplaced oversight.

Moreover, mission creep, according to Kevin Haggerty (2022) accompanies a general bureaucratic accretion of responsibilities, along with the hyper- cautious decisions that arise because of heightened fears of liability. Under those conditions, Gunsalus believes in expanding the review process to assess how regulations affect activities outside the framework, with the need to reconsider both conceptual and procedural aspects. This new vision "should identify activities that are/are not research requiring formal oversight, and should direct the development of new, written guidance" for ethics committees (Gunsalus 2003:1). Developed collaboratively across all non-biology disciplines, with a consistent and fair application, "it must be rooted in ethical principles, [and] fit the methodologies used in the humanistic disciplines." We must assume that the idea of humanistic disciplines includes the social sciences.

Rita McWilliams, a professor in a department of human ecology, Carl W. Hebden, an agricultural biotechnologist, and Adele M.K. Gilpin, an epidemiologist, all advocate a centralized system (McWilliams *et al.* 2006). In their view, there is an increasing number of studies that require substantially more varied expertise than is typically available for a proper evaluation. In addition to imposing a heavy burden on ethics committees, there is a lack of consistency as well as an uneven system of protection of research participants. A centralized review system would ensure that expert review is provided specific to the research at hand and maintain consistency in human subjects protection, all while reducing the time needed to obtain approval. Under such a system, members of ethics committees would remain at their respective institutions, taking advantage of remote communication technologies.

## 4. Entirely Doing Away with Research-Ethics Review Regime

The few critics who weigh in against any system of research-ethics review do so with a clear vision of the regulatory promiscuity brought on by the formal research-ethics regimes around the world. One idea involves doing away with the research-ethics governance structure entirely, as far as researchers in the social sciences are concerned.

Zachary M. Schrag (2011), a historian, has long made the point that, all too often, the process of ethical review overestimates fictitious or improbable dangers as a way of justifying the impositions and restrictions on all research. Schrag has always noted the problematic aspects of research-ethics review in the social sciences. It is quite customary for those who are not social science researchers to become extensively involved in contemporary debates about the very limited usefulness of research-ethics committees to researchers in the social sciences.

Carl E. Schneider (2015), professor of law and internal medicine, is a natural ally to the plight of these researchers. Iain Brassington (2016), a lecturer in bioethics, echoes Schrag's point of view that ethics committees tend to be too cautious, failing to take into account the vast range of activities and disciplines that make up the social sciences. As a consequence, they "lack a legible and convincing ethics" and "the autonomy of [ethics committees] means that they come to different decisions on identical cases" (Brassington 2016:69). Ethics committees "overemphasize informed consent, with the unintended consequence that cramming every possible eventuality into a consent form makes it utterly incomprehensible." Like those who agree with scholars in favour of abandoning research-ethics committees, Brassington portrays the regulationists as "a spooky band that seems to be composed of meddling do-gooders of whom all right-thinking people naturally disapprove."

Robert Dingwall, one of the sociologists who call for dismantling the research-ethics review regime, claims that, at its heart, the regime is "a process of censorship that is disabling to the democratic values by which we seek to live." Once we are able to recognize its vulnerability, "we need to deprive these bodies of the oxygen of legitimacy" (Dingwall 2006:57). Nathan Emmerich (2016), another sociologist, expresses a similar sentiment when he suggests that we should articulate a more positive vision of the social scientist's professional ethics. In this manner one can place the social sciences in their own moral and ethical place, with ethical practices that are inherent to the profession rather imposed upon it from outside. This approach rids social scientists of the "imperialism of a research ethics constructed for the purposes of governing biomedical research." As such the "moral equivalent" of the professions is "shared by the state and society as a whole" (Emmerich 2016:abstract). Emmerich argues that "social scientists should adopt a professional ethics" and suggests that a clinical ethics committee "might provide an alternative model for the governance of social science research." Paul Cloke *et al.* (2000:151) throw in a word of caution about the idea that researchers should somehow act in a manner ethically superior to that of ordinary people. Yet, if we really seek to avoid research as mere tourism—if we are serious about protecting research participants—then a more sustained and committed ownership of research as process, practice, and product seems to be required, especially in researching marginalized groups.

The second of the proposed ideas in this category ardently favours the notion of invoking a research-ethics covenant. This is probably the boldest idea. The origins of this idea are not clear but, like the practice of journalism, research ethics in the social sciences cannot be covered in a course.³ Each of the various disciplines within the social sciences has particular subfields that are either very distinctive or share some characteristics with a parallel field.

The notion of exercising a research covenant might touch every researcher's common faith that the issues of ethics in research lie not so much in compliance or control by an agency beyond the individual researcher. Rosa Castillo (2018:406) stresses that "there should be greater attention to the cultivation of ethical consciousness and behaviour among researchers through pedagogy and practice." The next chapter in *Seeking a Research-Ethics Covenant* explores the most salient aspects of exercising a research covenant.

Before delving into the idea of exercising a research covenant, I encourage the reader to turn to the Appendix to be apprised of the concrete differences in the way research in the social sciences is markedly different from that in medical fields of research. By way of summary, we see four essential ingredients that should distinguish the research process in much of sociology from the medical research-ethics paradigm: (a) closing the distance between the researcher and research participant; (b) acknowledging that the wide range of methods and research settings requires ethical nuances; (c) recognizing the role of the larger social and cultural contexts in the lives of research participants; and (d) the nurturing of human dignity as a significant focus of social researchers.

# 7

## Towards a New Approach
### *in the Social Sciences*

THIS FINAL CHAPTER offers a new approach to creating an ethical culture in research. It offers a diagnosis of the current stances in research ethics, and moreover, it asks what an integrated research-ethics culture looks like. The social sciences already have a research-ethics culture, which was in place before the imposition of the bioethics regime. To that end, this chapter adumbrates both general and specific solutions to the current dilemma, in which the bioethics regime has captured the practice of ethics in the social sciences. The principal thrust of this chapter invokes the benefits and possibilities associated with the use of a new ethics framework, namely a research-ethics covenant for the social sciences.

Researchers in the social sciences should be assured that *Seeking a Research-Ethics Covenant* does not advocate any layer of bureaucracy that now pervades auditing systems in the contemporary world. I hope to sketch a simpler and far less cumbersome system—one that does not require researchers to negotiate their way through a committee or ethics board in order to conduct their research ethically. This book offers, I hope, a new architecture.

## Diagnosis

From the outset, I have characterized contemporary research ethics in the social sciences as being in a state of crisis. That crisis, we suggest, rests on four pillars. One pillar involves an aggressive audit culture in universities. Another pillar consists of the privileged status of the medical research-ethics framework which creates yet another pillar that imprints that framework over all the other fields of scholarly endeavours. The fourth pillar, ironically, is put in place by a wide cadre of social researchers who recognize the dilemmas caused by the capture by the bioethics framework while disagreeing among themselves about the best way to resolve these dilemmas. We have touched on each of these pillars throughout various chapters in *Seeking a Research-Ethics Covenant*. These pillars are so interconnected that it would have made no sense to treat each one as if it is separate from the others. We normally assume that pillars represent something noble, but in this case, they represent a scourge and a blight on the way researchers in the social sciences conduct ethical research.

My colleague, Janice Ryan, shared in a personal email (February 13, 2021) her view that "after being wrapped in a legalistic/medicalistic process for so long…maybe the ethics boards have forgotten…the very sacred mutual relationship which can be quashed in power needs and models." Under the current conditions, the biomedical ethics model seems to have resulted in a loss of trust between the research participant and the researcher. As claimed elsewhere in this volume, the expectations of signing documents/consent forms, for example, serve the larger system of compliance and audits, not the participants. The current process does not acknowledge the perceptions or understanding of research participants; rather what is acknowledged is how institutions should perceive them.

Nichole Edwards (2018:328), relying on the work of Ann Oakley (2016), reminds us that some ethical considerations in the social sciences go against what social-science researchers "have been historically taught to maintain." Here is the rub: "if objectivity is the goal of 'good' research, you must only ever be a collector of data and, as such, detach yourself from the research process." In this perspective, when a researcher interviews someone, it is believed that it is the researcher who "will dictate the framework of dialogue, while the person answering questions is said to be relatively powerless... [T]he information passes one way."

Ethics committees have thus created a bifurcation between the practice of integrity in the field by researchers in the social sciences and the rule of ethics enshrined within a bureaucratic structure. The whole notion of "compliance" suggests something that stands outside of the thoughts and practices of individuals, whether they are participants or researchers.

Although their research methods render them unable to follow the codes laid down by the bioethics regime, researchers in the social sciences are still mandated to follow those codes. As a consequence, ethics committees view researchers in the social sciences as ethically promiscuous. Ethics committees are also inclined to believe that these researchers are nihilists, as far as ethical research is concerned. When the use of so-called ethics checklists come into play, many areas of research remain untouched, and the limitations articulated by these lists leave many areas of research open to inadvertent ethical conundrums. Even the relatively important cornerstone of doing ethical research, namely the idea of whether planned research constitutes a risk for participants, leaves us, according to my colleague Peter Weeks, with a list of unanswerable questions, conveyed to me via email and reproduced directly below.

For example: On what grounds can committee members claim to know the risks of the proposed research better than the researchers themselves? Do we wish to imply that these researchers cannot be trusted to assess the risks reliably? How can committee members claim to have superior knowledge of these risks? What would be the basis of such claims?

Moreover, the very rationale of such committees presupposes that researchers cannot be trusted to adhere to the relevant ethical guidelines. The work of the committees is based on what some have described as "the skeptical stance," such as the stance demanded of workers in social-assistance agencies whereby the applicants' claims are always to be perceived as biased, ill-founded, self-interested, *etc*. Essentially, the applicants are to be treated as guilty until proven innocent.

Finally, should the interrogations imposed by ethics committees be applied to themselves? Can we trust these people?! And why would we? They assume that, unlike mere researchers, they themselves could not be biased. Have they not been trained to be aware of the same ethical issues we expect the researchers to understand? How can they know that they know better? In addition, we can ask not only if the claims made by researchers are true but also whether they are trustworthy. Are the researchers being truthful in claiming any risks, and how would these committee members know that? (Peter Weeks, personal email to W. van den Hoonaard, July 23, 2021).[1]

My intent is to rediscover the ethical nuances that are an inherent part of qualitative research, believing that under the grip of current (medical) research-ethics regimes, many researchers have lost their way. The task of *Seeking a Research-Ethics Covenant* is to lay bare the conceptual labyrinth of research in the social sciences. Another task, thanks to the contribution by Dr. Marco Marzano, is to highlight the impact of the advent of formal ethics review on sociological research.

Social scientists are proficient in learning how to incorporate ethics into their research in ways that have proven to be both rigorous and relevant. Numerous studies on ethics in research emphasize the importance of reflection, or "honest self-reflexivity" (Cloke *et al.* 2000:150), according to which "reflexivity should not be confined to the production and interpretation stages of research but should also be employed in more all-embracing ethical evaluations of research…as they reach their conclusion."

## What Does an Integral Ethical Culture Look Like?

As odd as it may seem, recent tragic events in Nova Scotia triggered in me a thought that may well help us understand an approach to how a covenantal culture of research ethics can be brought about. The same process by which we attempt to bring about gender equality can be invoked to create an ethical process among social scientists.

The mass shooting of 22 individuals in April of 2020 in Nova Scotia, which centred around misogyny and violence towards women, alerted many of us to the urgent and long-term investments needed to socialize human beings in the process of creating an atmosphere of equality as the most enduring way to eliminate the abuse of women by men. Women's emergency shelters, of course, cannot disappear overnight, as they remain a much-needed service to assist those escaping violence by men. However, it is not hard to imagine that creating equality should be a lifelong effort on everyone's part. If all aspects of society—schools at all levels in the educational system, along with various informal and formal venues, as well as families—inculcate every child with the idea that there is no place for violence or abuse in an ethos of equality, we would eventually experience the rise of gender equality. One can venture to guess that instances of abuse would eventually be eliminated. That ethos should obviously be ever-present in our lives. One could draw on that analogy to instill a profound sense of ethics as one's professional ethos. Sociologists are well aware of the notion of public issues versus private problems. What prevents the resolution of private problems is the lack of awareness that such problems need to be seen as public issues.

One can imagine a professional setting where prospective professional researchers in the social sciences are so well versed in all aspects of ethics and integrity in research that ethics committees would become redundant. Under the current circumstances, social researchers are induced to follow guidelines in ethics codes that are so specific that the researchers can become regarded as ethics *flâneurs*.

Invoking a research covenant allows the social researcher to escape the mandatory entanglement in research-ethics codes, whether in North America or elsewhere. What stands in front of us is perhaps the boldest and yet the least assuming task in creating a culture that can nurture and sustain ethical approaches to doing research in the social sciences. A research-ethics covenant calls for affirming an ethos of integrity in our professional lives. To develop such an ethos, one needs to be immersed in it from the very start of one's professional training.

I am of the opinion that the idea of a research-ethics covenant will constitute a progressive development—a move from standing under the wing of the patriarchal legal/medical model to claiming one's own ethical voice and professional and ethical standards in the social sciences. This is what a new architecture calls for, according to Rosa Castillo (2018), a socio-cultural anthropologist and assistant professor at Humboldt University Berlin's Department for Southeast Asian Studies. It was Dr. Castillo's mother, Fatima Alvarez Castillo, who shaped her knowledge of research ethics (Rosa Castillo, personal email to W. van den Hoonaard, April 20, 2020). Her mother was a feminist political scientist and a retired researcher in the medical and social sciences who wished to make the ethics-review process compatible with the particularities and complexities of qualitative research. In her view, beyond the formal requirements of the ethics-review committee, research ethics is a matter of praxis. Dr. Castillo started to learn about research ethics as a little girl by watching her mother give workshops and training on the subject for village and municipal health workers and for researchers in various parts of the Philippines. Her approach makes sense in every aspect—an approach that is durable and self-sustaining, requiring no overhead structure to oversee it. She advocates abandoning the formalized ethics-review system and proposes a more responsive process to arrive at better-informed decisions about the ethical quality and thrust of social research.

## The Social Sciences as Home of Research Ethics

What is curious is that researchers in the social sciences have long been aware of the various ethical conundrums in their fields of research, but the biomedical ethics paradigm has silenced their voices. The approach advocated here is *not* about teaching an occasional course on ethics in research. It is more integrative than that; it is about making ethics an integral part of the professional curriculum and/or training.

Previous chapters have described the historical paths of ethics in anthropology and sociology. What stands out with respect to the ethics histories of both disciplines is their close connection to the force of American involvement in world affairs. In sociology, the world was (and perhaps still is) quite enamoured with the principles promoted by the US Office for Human Research Protections. In anthropology, the very founding and evolution of this discipline are premised on its close ties to the United States and its worldwide influence.

The current chapter outlines this final task, namely the adoption of an ethics covenant. We are eager to draw on the work of Rosa Castillo as the conceptual home of a research-ethics covenant. The world of anglophone anthropology (and subsequently, social research in general) has become seriously short-circuited by "increased bureaucratization, audit and rigidity and an incompatibility with the ethnographic method" (Castillo 2018:406). Castillo brings out two essential points. On one hand, the current, formalized research-ethics process is contradictory to the epistemology and methodology of anthropology, and, more broadly, of the social sciences. On the other hand, the current system does not necessarily guarantee that research will be conducted in an ethical manner. We need to recognize that in the social sciences, many decisions involving ethics have to be made on the fly in the throes of research. Deborah K. van den Hoonaard, as social-science editor of a Canadian academic journal, found that many authors are unable to think of ethical considerations beyond compliance (personal communication). The prohibition on students conducting research as part of a class project may have precluded any learning about how to make ethical decisions in the course of these projects.

In the face of routine research-ethics review in the academy, the faint of heart may well have second thoughts about distilling the essence of research ethics in the social sciences. Braver souls will see an opportunity to propound the benefits of conducting social research within a new ethics framework. These same souls have already faced numerous critics who have valued research that was hypothesis-driven and highlighted causal research.

It may come down to doing "discovery" research—that is, research that opens new lines of inquiry not based on preliminary assumptions—as opposed to the more hypothesis-driven "affirmatory" approach that is characteristic of quantitative research.

Before the arrival of research-ethics committees, as attested by Marco Marzano,

> [s]ociologists have always managed ethical issues in an implicit way. Think of Goffman (1961). He did terrific covert research at St. Elisabeth Hospital. No informed consent, no ethics control from IRBs, nothing of this stuff, but certainly he is thought to have done ethical research, writing a book on how a total institution affected inmates' lives…Personally, I think, and I am sure that you agree with me, that his ethnographic work was much more ethical than thousands of boring and empty ethnographies written during the era of ethical regulation and passed under the yoke of an IRB. (personal email to W. van den Hoonaard, April 13, 2020)

Aside from breaking free from the shackles of a medical perspective on research ethics, the ethics revolution must also attend to the bureaucratic structures that are extensions of the medical ethics paradigm. Virtually every country in the world is in thrall to that American framework, creating ambiguities for researchers in the social sciences. Contradictions, detailed research plans, cultural complexities of doing research, and interpretations all seem to disappear magically from the boardrooms of research-ethics committees, much to the chagrin of researchers in the social sciences and the humanities.

The only responsible answer can be found, according to Castillo, when there is "greater attention to the cultivation of ethical consciousness and behaviour among researchers through pedagogy and practice" (Castillo 2018:406). This approach nurtures a researcher's "capacity to make ethical decisions and actions and make ethical thinking and acting a fundamental part of all stages of our research and engagements." Such an approach makes ethics "part of our reflexivity and consciousness in all stages of our research practice" (Castillo 2018:407). The vastness of topics and methods embedded in social-science research should enable all to absorb and benefit from past experiences as reported in the literature. While no doubt ethical awareness can be imagined as mirrors, gems, or pearls, it should also be brought to mind that these are dynamic, not static, facets of learning about ethics, and that mirrors need dusting, gems require polishing, and pearls need to be lustrous rather than dull. As Christopher Buck (1998) asserts, these are not ends unto themselves but require refinements that prove the worth of such mirrors, gems, and pearls.

What prevails in any reflection about research ethics and research-ethics review is the seemingly unalterable and pervasive influence of social and political structures. *Seeking a Research-Ethics Covenant* has already unearthed the powerful impact of university audit cultures, the extensive privilege assigned to biomedical ethics codes in determining the shape of research, for example, by Dr. Castillo, a scholar originally from the Philippines. We have seen how, in the case of anthropology, the United States' role in the world has also shaped the principles of ethics codes of sociology. Moreover, the broad range of countervailing insights among scholars' proposed remedies could lead one to despair about finding any solutions at all.

*Seeking a Research-Ethics Covenant* therefore took on two tasks. The first was to argue for the entire abandonment of the medical research-ethics model as the prescriptive guide for researchers in the social sciences. The second was to prompt us to ask ourselves how we can replace that particular model. This task requires us to re-envision the bureaucratic structures used to tether non-medical research to the framework of ethical research from a medical standpoint. How do we go forward? The proffered remedies (as outlined in Chapter Six) do not provide much guidance. It is telling that researchers whose backgrounds consist of training in the social sciences are generally in favour of proposals that get rid of any institutional involvement with research-ethics review. That approach is a better fit for the temperament of those researchers and the nature of their craft.

Chapter Six offered eight sets of proposals to carry ethical research forward in the modern world (with these proposals sorted into four major categories). Throughout, *Seeking a Research-Ethics Covenant* has tried to correlate each set of proposals with the disciplinary backgrounds of their advocates. The most stringent proposals, as few as they are, recommend that ethics codes be tightened, especially with regard to the informed-consent process. Would it be fair to say that the concerns of researchers in the social sciences are not evident in this set of proposals? Individuals from the fields of social epidemiology, psychology, and social welfare subscribe to this approach. If there is a challenge, it is to create a revolution in the ethics-review system that will allow for the emergence of ethical concepts that are meaningful and relevant for those working in such disciplines as the social sciences, oral history, feminist research, and so on.

Another set of proposals advocates significant changes in how members of ethics committees themselves should deliberate about the research proposals that come across their desks. This category of proposals, in comparison to all others, carries the weight of being the most popular choice. Its advocates span a range of both academic and professional fields: bioethics, sociology, psychology, philosophy, education, social welfare, anthropology, law, and occupational therapy. Missing from this list is the field of medicine.

It is noteworthy that those who see the benefits of either establishing a new regime or a split in regulatory control (*i.e.*, medical research versus non-medical research) are grounded in the fields of law, human ecology, biotechnology, epidemiology, theatre arts (drama), psychoanalysis, and gerontology. Faced with the persistent existence of ethics committees for the past 30 years or so, proponents of this approach may have found it more fruitful and beneficial to argue for considerable change *within* the current structure. Many would find this approach appealing for that reason alone.

The following section touches on matters that deserve the kind of ethical reflection that a covenant can easily sustain. However, we always need to remind ourselves that any solution to these issues must be arrived at through reflection and thoughtful action by the researcher—not through a top-down approach with pre-formulated answers. Ethical issues must be addressed by researchers, either through consultation with colleagues or by delving into the research literature. As it turns out, the distinctive approach based on Indigenous research practices that we discussed earlier can be a useful guide.

In light of the many limitations placed by ethics committees in their attempts to guide researchers, it is clear that new insights are needed to further the cause of sustaining the ethical dimensions of research in the social sciences. Here, I offer the notion of a research-ethics covenant as a novel contribution to the field of research ethics.

# Towards a Research-Ethics Covenant

Throughout time we have found multiple meanings of a covenant. On a broader scale one merely has to turn to the pages of history to unravel its ancient uses, going back to Mosaic law. A covenant constitutes a "formal alliance or agreement...with humanity in general" (Anonymous 2023). On a smaller scale, a covenant can cement interpersonal and wider societal relations in a binding agreement. The covenant acquires a solemn character. It can apply to several areas of human action. A research-ethics covenant deals particularly with the idea of committing oneself to ethics in conducting research.

Although the concept of a research-ethics covenant has, by itself, a short history, the notion of a covenant has a long, deeply valued, and respectable legacy in religion. In Western and other cultures, a covenant is firmly tied to, for example, the Jewish idea of ethics and morality. Some, like Malcolm Fraser (2014), attest that "there is a common ethic running through the world's major religions." It has a path that spans a long time. Covenantal thinking is also buried in biblical thought and constitutes the warp and woof of theological thought and action in religions that stand outside of strictly Jewish or Christian parameters, such as in Islam (Moghimi 2019; Schimmel 1994) or in the Baháʼí Dispensation (more recently founded in 1844), where it is the essential frame of reference for the continuity of that religion (Buck 1998). The attachment to a covenant has strengthened the notions of morality and ethics and has permeated the thinking of such leading thinkers as Karl Barth (Selinger 1998). Throughout many cultures, covenantal ethics can also be interpersonal. It is a moral force that undergirds religious beliefs where the deity is one party in the relationship and humans are the other. The idea of covenantal ethics has found expression in numerous contemporary fields and practices. Randi Rashkover (2017) has found that elections contain a niche for covenantal ethics. The fields of nursing (Cooper 1988; Fowler 2017), of clinical work and contemporary medicine (Rusthoven 2014), of corporate or business activities, of pharmacists, of legal practices (Allegretti 1998), and of archival practices (Cline 2012) have all found their footing in a quasi-religious framework. Legal enforcement may well underpin these assumptions, but their foundation is the moral commitment to uphold them. We need to remind ourselves that, as Matthew D. Viel (2001) notes, individuals do not lead stagnant, dead lives. Rather, they are immersed in living systems that are maintained by assumptions. We humans are not simple, isolated individuals but lead dynamic lives within a cultural and historical context. It has always made sense for humans to immerse themselves in covenantal ethics, a living system of human relations.

There are many equivalents to the idea of covenants in other cultures and languages. Covenants point to a *sacred relationship.* When, for example, Perry Robinson speaks of the Navajo context, the term "relationship" denotes

> the complexity of Navajo thought about the world we live in... The creation story is filled with animate beings who interacted with each other as they established patterns to guide the Navajo in proper behavior. Rocks, rivers, trees, animals, and even diseases have powers within that can be prayed to for assistance. Also in the beginning, the clan system began to evolve, resulting in today's approximately ninety clans, an important part of the tribe's growing population...[T]here is no reason for any Navajo

to feel alone and depressed since the people and their world
are filled with many different types of friendly relationships.
(Perry Robinson 2019)

As holdovers from the past, covenants are, by their nature, sacred. What stands out today is the dual nature of covenants: an ethical responsibility to others and to ourselves. Covenantal ethics incorporates elements of voluntariness and commitment to action—an ideal approach when distancing oneself from a previous path of action such as reliance on ethics committees. All of that requires stamina.

Attachment to a covenant thus "carries moral weight" (Maiter *et al.* 2008:308). Commitment to stewardship and integrity is crucial. It is a civic engagement. This moral reasoning is part of a broad, normative covenantal tradition where duty, virtue, and responsibility are inextricably tied together in a mutually reinforcing manner, and where the organizational setup has a covenantal quality.

One might well ask how such an approach could fit into the manner of conducting contemporary ethical research. A dedicated effort by researchers, with the help of their institutions, to foster the idea of promoting a research-ethics covenant could go a long way to moving decisions about research ethics out of the warren of contest, competition, and confrontation.

It might be a challenge to convince contemporary Western (mostly secular) researchers of this idea. We have to ask ourselves whether the idea of a covenant fits into our secular culture. The next paragraphs explain what the germane features of a covenant are, and to what extent the issue of ethics in research can call upon such a covenant to guide researchers through to ethical research.

Human life is relational and thus human interaction should be the centre of attention for both scientific and ethical reasons. Norwegian researcher Anne Inga Hilsen (2006:69) states that it is through our practice as researchers that we "live our ethics." She illustrated her position by referring to her experiences over three years (2003–2005) with an organizational development project in the National Insurance Service (NIS) in Norway. As an action researcher, she challenged herself to identify the grounding of her research practice, which dealt with industrial relations. She started to realize that human interdependency, the cogeneration of knowledge, and greater justice in power relations should be the bases of her research. She strongly believes that it is through her scientific practice that she demonstrates her ethical foundation.

The attachment to a covenant, however, should be seen in a broader contemporary context, substantially dictating moral and ethical facets of life, including the realm of ethics in research. The notion of attachment to a covenant is not an interim solution or approach. A covenantal approach to ethics in research permits the researcher to see beyond the instantaneous and immediate requirement of ethics when facing critical moments in research.

A covenantal approach gives researchers an opportunity to envision the drama of ethical research throughout their entire lives, including in moments of teaching ethics to the next generation. One can already see the urgent need for two things: the disassembling of the organizational framework of committees, and a commitment to stewardship and integrity on the part of researchers. Armed with the force of relevant knowledge and ethical sensibilities, emerging scholars would be fully involved with "all acts of representation and engagement" (Castillo 2018:407), based on practical and theoretical lessons from the field and from studies or research in the social sciences.

Beginning in one's undergraduate years, this ethical praxis will sustain a lifelong habit that is "tested and reshaped in every aspect and stage of a scholar's work" (Castillo 2018:406). In due course, the formalization and bureaucratization of ethics can give way to the more sustaining ideas related to the particularities and complexities of our disciplines. One should expect slight variations of this process across different countries, according to the research-ethics structure in each country. In some countries, researchers might be inclined to consult "research interlocutors" who have special expertise on the ethical issues in their field. One might see such consultations as a viable alternative to going through a bureaucratic structure that is steeped in the thinking of medical ethics.

It is, I suggest, an approach that links together duty, virtue, and responsibility. It obliges a researcher to embrace ethical approaches in their field of research. It guarantees integrity. The realities of the social world necessitate researchers to be cognizant of the idea that "people in all societies are bound to one another in basic social exchanges that consolidate social relationships, ranging from marriage and kinship in small-scale societies to complex economic transactions among global trading partners" (Maiter *et al.* 2008:307). The exigencies of informal groups, whether small or large, express the same mode of social exchange. The study of research settings cannot go forward without taking into account all these exigencies and without resorting to focussing on a covenant that ties the individual researcher to a deeper sense of social exchange. In effect, all research in that sense is "participatory," at whatever level the researcher engages with the group or individuals being studied.

The key notion of being an ethical researcher is not about exhibiting compliance to an external institutional machinery. It is about instilling in the researcher the sense that deeply ingrained ethical conduct is like being bound by a covenant—a sacred or hallowed trust if you will. An example of this is the context of the Arctic research of my daughter, Lisa-Jo van den Scott, and her husband, Jeffrey. At a later stage in the research, the Elders of the community (Arviat), who had become well acquainted with their work, gave their wholehearted approval to the project and urged them to share their findings with others beyond the community. Lisa-Jo and Jeff van den Scott regarded that approval as a sacred trust, a covenant. We can find the same covenantal assumptions behind various other facets of contemporary life, even if we may not have thought of them in that particular light; an implicit covenant is at work in prohibitions on smoking, in the ingrained agreement in many countries to drive on the right side of the road, in the move towards fostering the equality of women and men, in standing up for the rights of the Māori, and so on.

Several researchers, especially Anne Inga Hilsen (2006; 2014) and Mary Brydon-Miller (2009; 2011; 2013), have already given practical thought to the importance of covenantal ethics to action research and community-based research practices.

At a higher level of decision making, departments in the relevant disciplines will ideally eventually distance themselves from the concerns and evaluations of research-ethics committees. This distancing could take place as a measured transition. A university might decide to initiate this process as an experiment, and later adopt it as a more enduring aspect of the university or institution once the new approach is sturdy enough. Academic departments could evaluate this period of transition away from the existing medical model of research before arriving at a final decision. Undergraduate (and graduate) programs could readjust their ethical lenses when introducing research in the social sciences among their required courses; when this approach satisfies a department, every effort can be made, as laid out by Castillo (2018), to satisfy the criteria of the university and any national offices established for the protection of humans in research (in Canada, for example, this would be the Panel on Research Ethics).

However, in implementing this approach, the university will need to allot the kind of time that researchers in the social sciences need. *Seeking a Research-Ethics Covenant* has repeatedly emphasized the need to exercise the virtue of patience when researchers conduct ethnographic or qualitative work.

The process of instilling ethical reflection does not necessarily focus on an individual student, but rather on a coterie of students and other scholars, so that inculcating knowledge of ethics in research is more far-reaching. Exposing students and scholars to ethical practices and behaviour through examples in social-science research will encourage them to move beyond local contextual thinking. This is particularly relevant because ethics committees generally do not allow students to try out research methods in classes. As a result, they have no practical introduction into doing ethical research. None at all. Acquainting both new and veteran scholars with the rich and deep literature on what can be learned about research ethics across the board of the social sciences (which is part of learning about a research covenant) leads researchers to understand the workings of research ethics in many different contexts. This approach guides researchers away from particular local contexts of research.

The covenantal approach works under the assumption of reciprocity and balance of power. Does the payment of research participants pertain only to the expenses that research participants incur? No less significant an issue relates to the pronouncement of findings by the researcher of uncomfortable truths—truths that may offend the people with whom we (as scholars) are doing research. Such an action performed by the researcher can be considered ethically appropriate only if it is done not with the intention of harming someone, but with the intention of announcing to a friend (the research participant) something that the friend does not want to know.

At this stage, one might want to explore some of the other distinct advantages of holding fast to a research-ethics covenant and consider relevant issues. Don Reynolds (2000) makes a number of suggestions, the most relevant being the need to strengthen an inherent interest in the salient features of research in the social and behavioural sciences that "will reduce the tensions...and will better protect the subjects [sic] of social and behaviour studies." A research-ethics covenant can reduce or eliminate the acerbic relations that currently attend the world of research-ethics policies. All too often, contests, competitions, and confrontations discourage the fruitful use of energy, commitment, and time (of both researchers and ethics committee members). The capital-intensive, market-driven, competitive approach, where researchers work at breakneck speed, needs to be surrendered to the thoughtful processes attached to what researchers in the social sciences really do.

Just as research participants fall under the influence of their culture, so too do researchers who work within academic circles. They face an academic (and public) culture that valorizes individualism, one-upmanship, and social prestige, often attached to material rewards. Other systemic and social factors probably interact in varying combinations over the course of research activities, further entrenching these difficulties. Competition for scarce research funding, rivalries among academic disciplines, the economic power of the biomedical industries, and the high esteem granted to STEM subjects are all dynamics that exist to varying degrees in the politics of contemporary universities. There is also a growing preponderance of indices and impact factors—such as the *h-index* or the *i10-index*—that exacerbate all of the above.

It would be a surprise if such influences did not exert themselves, whether consciously or subliminally, in ethics reviews (Bond 2012). No researchers who pride themselves on ethical reflection can ignore these influences. Researchers make decisions that relate not only to the acquisition of grants or funds for their research, but also in regard to publishing, which may have both short-term and long-term effects. Integrity in research also extends to relationships of trust with colleagues and students.

Moreover, we cannot ignore other contemporary covenantal elements that have taken hold in some quarters of society. These assumptions are sometimes negatively laden, expressing themselves as deeply held belief systems, typically related to class, status, caste, or other identifiable social hierarchies. There is no reason to assume that these covenantal understandings cannot pertain to the other social realms of ethics, behaviour and conduct, and policy. These latter beliefs touch the profound sentiments of fighting racism, promoting environmental issues, or being committed to the principle of the oneness of humanity.

There are additional pivots that sustain a covenant on research ethics. "Reciprocity" write Sarah Maiter *et al.* (2008:305), is as "an ongoing process of exchange with the aim of establishing and maintaining equality between parties," while exploring "how this notion might inform our understanding of the ethical implications of…[our own] research."

This approach opens up several avenues for the affirmation of a covenant. A departmental panel might consider evaluating the courses and materials that are used to equip students with knowledge about ethics. Courses are probably not the ideal vehicle for transmitting ethical thought. The evaluation of a student's ethical sensibilities could instead proceed following an alternative structured manner. Rosa Castillo (2018:407) suggests that colleagues might together explore a student's "positionality, responsibilities, and accountabilities during and after research" in a pedagogical process guided by a competent panel. She avers that a researcher's identity should not be defined in terms of data management, but should be related to whether the researcher is cognizant of a wide spectrum of research approaches (Castillo 2018). The format of this process is informal, resembling perhaps a barrel of ideas on research ethics accumulated by colleagues and students.

A research covenant would strengthen the potential for creating the kind of ethical research that would benefit all. *Seeking a Research-Ethics Covenant* advocates the idea of invoking a research covenant that would be sufficient in instilling ethical consciousness in all researchers in the social sciences.

Will some university—perhaps the first one to begin on truly cultivating ethical researchers—be brave enough to embark on this new approach to instilling ethical sensibilities in its cadre of scholars and students? Would a covenantal approach not be better at resolving ethical dilemmas in the field? Ethics committees around the world are not particularly noted for their adventurous spirit, but the situation of research ethics is dire, particularly for the social sciences. It may well be the only way to avoid the current ethics disorder that arises when researchers in the social sciences are mandated to adhere to the reigning biomedical framework and its various codes, policies, and ethics committees.

# Appendix

## *The New Brunswick Declaration on Research Ethics, Integrity, and Governance*

### Introduction

Despite their growth and extension of power, overworked ethics review committees are limping along.[1] Many have commented on the structural problems of the regime: the inability of ethics committees to make consistent decisions (Dziak *et al.* 2005; O'Neill 2016), the inability of ethics committees, despite their local strength, to effect any necessary policy changes, and the long periods of abeyance for national agencies to bring about essential amendments in ethics codes. Other scholars (some are listed in endnote 3) have found other weaknesses in the system. Finally, the costs are astronomical (Dingwall 2016; Whitney and Schneider 2011).

This chapter explores the need for research-ethics review committees to nurture and maintain ethical relations with researchers.[2] First, the chapter explores the unbalanced spread of ethical obligations imposed by Canada's *TCPS* (*i.e.*, the *Tri-Council Policy Statement: Ethical Conduct for Research Involving Humans*; see CIHR *et al.* 2014; 2018) on individual REB members and on researchers, respectively. This imbalance shows that ethical relations with researchers are not the primary consideration in *TCPS*; ethical imperatives for individual REB members and for researchers are so divergent that it is difficult to build ethical relationships between the two stakeholders. It then discusses *The New Brunswick Declaration on*

*Research Ethics, Integrity, and Governance* resulting from the First Ethics Rupture Summit, held in October 2012 in Fredericton, New Brunswick. The *Declaration* is one of the most recent formal expressions of the need for such ethical relations (van den Hoonaard 2013d).

The disquiet around research-ethics codes is having a profound effect on the conduct of research, especially in the social sciences. Since before 2000, an estimated 335–350 articles have appeared in the social science literature that describe in agonizing detail how research-ethics codes are missing the mark as far as the social sciences are concerned.[3] Numerous are also the key journals that include articles which point to this pervasive dislocation of the social sciences.[4] We also witness the publication of books and the holding of conferences that underscore the problematic nature of the ethics regime for social scientists. Some propose the full abandonment of these codes, partly because many academic societies already have well-established ethics practices; others offer piecemeal solutions.

Many researchers in the social sciences have fully surrendered themselves to the inevitability of needing to comply with formal ethics codes. They are even using the language and terminologies more common in the biomedical and clinical-trial fields rather than those used in the social sciences themselves. Some argue that this trend portends a form of colonization by the medical sciences at the expense of the culture of the social sciences (van den Hoonaard 2014a; Humphreys *et al.* 2014).

One cannot but help notice the relentless process of students narrowing their research sights to the strictures of ethics codes in a manner that is both frustrating and often quite unhelpful to them. However, it is ironic that with their emphasis on protecting people in vulnerable contexts, ethics committees (IRBs in the United States and REBs in Canada) overlook the fact that students are *de facto* a vulnerable population.

## Uneven Disbursement of Ethical Obligations

Many problems with the ethics regime stem from the fact that ethics committees do not see themselves as ethical agents. Rather, they see themselves as enforcers who are keen to compel researchers to follow rule-bound decisions of committees—hardly a condition for an ethical relationship (Bledsoe et al. 2007; Bond 2012; Bosk 2007; Bosk and De Vries 2004; Carr 2015; Shaul 2002). Moreover, ethics codes demand more from researchers insofar as personal virtues are concerned. Canada's research-ethics policy, *TCPS* 2 (CIHR et al. 2018), contains thirteen chapters. My analysis of the spread of personal virtues only takes into account *TCPS* 2's general chapters (*i.e.*, 1 to 8) because those chapters affect all researchers and REB members, regardless of discipline or topic. The chapters contain 136 mandatory provisions for all parties who have a stake in implementing *TCPS* 2. The document contains 514 "shoulds." Of the 136 ethical provisions,[5] *TCPS* 2 spells out no fewer than 88 ethical provisions for researchers (almost two-thirds of the total). At the other extreme—and no less intriguing—is the fact that individual members of ethics committees are bound by only two ethical provisions, which appear in the chapter on Conflicts of Interest. Such a divergent weight of ethical principles is bound to produce strains and ruptures in the system. This imbalance of virtues (*i.e.*, what is expected of individual committee members and of individual researchers) and the paucity of ethical obligations imposed on REB members drive home even further the dissatisfaction researchers feel towards REBs in general.

Who, indeed, is inclined to follow ethical provisions, which are relatively absent from the mandated conduct of ethics committee members but fully set out for researchers? The United States code (Office for Human Research Protections 2008) is no different.[6] It spells out at least 22 ethical imperatives for researchers (a number of them are dressed up as research directives); only one is directed at individual members of IRBs (§46.107) and that one pertains to conflicting interests. The presentation of qualifications of these members (§46.103.3) makes no mention of any virtues or ethical principles that each should be noted for, such as fair dealings with researchers and students, or valuing methodological diversity. We now turn our attention to the *The New Brunswick Declaration on Research Ethics, Integrity, and Governance*, which was created out of a deep concern about this imbalance.

# The New Brunswick Declaration on Ethics in Research

Over 30 scholars from around the world convened in Fredericton, Canada, on 25–28 October 2012, to collectively consider the diminishment of the social sciences as a result of the growing number of ethics codes and regimes proliferating around the world. Known as the "Ethics Rupture Summit," this gathering explored new ways of understanding and addressing the fundamental problems of ethics regimes.[7] Its end-document, the *New Brunswick Declaration*, not only expressed the well-considered sentiments of these researchers, but also set out a simple, but radical solution: members of ethics committees should treat researchers in the same way that they expect researchers to treat research participants.

Until recently, the main force of complaints by social scientists was the use of the biomedical paradigm to articulate research-ethics codes. This paradigm has been found wanting, seriously so. Increasingly, what captures the essence of ethics regimes is the need to see them as enterprises of control and enforcement. In that connection, the *New Brunswick Declaration* highlights the need to view relations between ethics committees and researchers as ethical.[8] In matters of research-ethics governance, is it not logical that those relations with researchers be ethical?

The *New Brunswick Declaration* highlights a number of significant points. The *Declaration* explicitly connects to the *Universal Declaration of Human Rights* and extends ethical principles beyond the regulatory culture of ethics regimes, in particular, the right to freedom of expression, the right to conduct research, and the right of researchers to be respected, not demonized.[9] Robert Dingwall (2016:38) sees a tight connection among these rights, but social scientists pay an entry price "with the spread of pre-emptive regulation." The ecology of the social sciences is being disrupted in ways that may not be beneficial. As ethics regulation directs social science research away from "difficult" populations, topics, and methods, it creates systematic areas of ignorance about social conditions. Without such knowledge, however, it is difficult to create the transparency among people that promotes better lives. Creative artists and journalists, often seen as the pillars of democratic societies, are not subject to such pre-emptive regulation and therefore do not pay the same cost for expression.

What stands out in the *Declaration* is the value placed on the relevance of collectivities and communities, which the term "persons" as individuals does not sufficiently convey. Society is not an aggregate of individuals. As I claim (van den Hoonaard 2013a:24), society constitutes "a pattern of social action, [and] a culture that requires its own approach and method of analysis." The implications are more far-reaching than one realizes at first. Is it, for example, futile to seek individual informed consent? Researchers can learn from the practices of Indigenous researchers on how community consent is actualized.

The idea of privileging benefit over risk strikes at the root of many taken-for-granted assumptions about ethics in research. The uncertainties and risks associated with medical research take on a different hue in social research, where one does not find the same intense risk as in medical research. The idea of privileging benefit over risk in research "communicates the importance of not having research stray too far from its essential purpose: to bring benefits" (van den Hoonaard 2013a:25).

The *Declaration* believes that professional codes of ethical practice are highly relevant. One needs to move away "from beneath the shadow of a bureaucracy" (van den Hoonaard 2013a:25) and the obsession to maintain compliance. Research-ethics practices will thus gain a new life, beyond the usual culprits: checklists and standardization across a broad spectrum of research (Goldacre 2008). A true scholar acknowledges diversity and flexibility of ethical practices, as reflected below in items of the *Declaration*.

*Appendix*

*The New Brunswick Declaration: A Declaration on Research Ethics, Integrity, and Governance*

1. Seeks to promote respect for the right to freedom of expression;
2. Affirms that the practice of research should respect persons and collectivities and privilege the possibility of benefit over risk;
3. Believes researchers must be held to professional standards of competence, integrity, and trust; encourages regulators and *administrators to nurture a regulatory culture that grants researchers the same level of respect that researchers should offer research participants;*
4. Seeks to promote the social reproduction of ethical communities of practice;
5. Is committed to ongoing critical analysis of new and revised ethics regulations and regimes;
6. Shall work together to bring new experience, insights, and expertise to bear on these principles, goals, and mechanisms.

*February 4, 2013*

There are not many scholarly publishing venues left that do not require a formal acknowledgement that the research has "passed ethics." Such a mention has become a trite exercise and reveals not much about the intricacies of doing ethical research. I refer to this system of up-and-down linkages of ethics approval as "vertical ethics" (van den Hoonaard 2011; see also Srivastava 2011; van den Scott 2016; Edwards *et al.* 2004; Fistein and Quilligan 2012). The system of vertical ethics can produce less than desirable results. The home IRB might approve the ethics of the research, but a journal might still foreclose on the publication of an article, using an ethics temperature gauge that is at odds with the original basis of approval. The *Declaration* argues that vertical ethics holds many problems without making the research (or the publication of such research) more ethical.

The *Declaration* introduced a principle that is stunning in its simplicity: why shouldn't ethics committees afford researchers the same respect as ethics committees expect researchers to show towards research participants? The *Declaration* argues that the conventional, adversarial relations between ethics committees and researchers should be transmuted into an ethically more viable relationship (Fost and Levine 2007; Garrard and Dawson 2005; Jamrozik and Kolybaba 1999; Minnis 2004).

There is a longing, whether inside the formal ethics regime or outside of it, that students as upcoming scholars get a taste of what ethical research is like. It is hard to know how ethics in research can be taught. When ethics staff are invited to teach about ethics, the predominant approach addresses how to prepare ethics applications and forms—hardly a matter of teaching students how to reflect on ethics in research (van den Hoonaard 2002; 2006b; 2013d). The CITI (Collaborative Institutional Training Initiative) comes to mind, but there are enough criticisms of this ethics-testing method to suggest that it is relatively meaningless (Srivastava 2011; van den Scott 2016). Students (and faculty) have found ways to circumvent the test either by using split or alternate screens on their computer. It appears though that the one thing that CITI inadvertently teaches is cynicism. There are too few questions in the CITI that actually show what research is like in the social sciences (van den Hoonaard 2014b). There is no replacement for "strong mentoring, experiential learning, and nurturance" to "engage students and novice researchers with ethics in research settings" (van den Hoonaard 2013a:26).

Social scientists—by outlook, training, and practice—are accustomed to challenging taken-for-granted issues, both in their teaching and research. There are plenty of university courses that cast a critical eye upon racism, urban blight, gender, intellectual history, and so on. No area of human endeavour is exempt from thoughtful and critical analyses. The one obvious exception is ethics-policy conferences, where one very seldom hears such analyses. There is much to be gained from hearing contrary points of view. A course critical of the university's ethics committees would, in the end, create an understanding and acceptance of ethics policies. Off campus, social scientists feel a high sense of discomfort when such conferences are really *faits accomplis* engineered by agencies that intend to promote acceptance of new policies. Bubble-wrapped, these gatherings offer no means of placing ethics policies under a microscope (van den Hoonaard and Hamilton 2016). The *Declaration* urges the incorporation of critical and scholarly analysis as a significant feature of such gatherings. At the same time, the *Declaration* promulgates the idea that every gathering should not only include the importance of "highlighting exemplary and innovative research ethics review processes; [but also] identifying tensions and contradictions among various elements of research ethics governance" (van den Hoonaard 2013a:27).

Without any formal institutions promoting the *New Brunswick Declaration*, it is anyone's speculation how far this document will resonate within the ethics sectors. It represents a move away from the bureaucratic structure of the current ethics regimes and posits an ethical relationship between ethics committees and researchers (Whitney 2012; Wynn 2016). The current ethics regimes may have already travelled too far and invested too much energy and resources to undergo an ethical turnaround in how business is conducted. The hope for change relies heavily on the notion that social change is often abrupt—witness the Berlin Wall's sudden and unheralded collapse, for example. When we turn our vision skyward, we see flocks of birds changing their flight course at a moment's notice.

Can we speculate that changes in the research-ethics codes can be as sudden? A future paper may well discuss the influence that ethical relationships between REBs and researchers will have on research.

# Notes

## 1 | The Climate of Research-Ethics Review in the Social Sciences

1. The United Nations now formally recognizes the term "Indigenous" although some individuals, such as researcher Cindy Blackstock, prefer a more nuanced and specific approach—she notes that the term "Indigenous" lacks distinctness.
2. I was fortunate to have met Ms. Murdena Marshall in an introductory sociology class I was teaching in her community on Cape Breton Island in 1980.
3. As a practical aside, *Seeking a Research-Ethics Covenant* often uses "ethics committees" to refer to "research-ethics committees." Particular segments of the book speak of "IRBs" in reference to institutional review boards (in the United States). Each country has its own designation for such committees, but the term "ethics committees" is the generic reference I use in this book.

## 2 | A Robust Audit Culture and Its Aversion to Diversity

1. These are annual conferences held in Canada for the purpose of acquainting all researchers with the nature and purpose of qualitative research.

## 3 | The Capture of the Social Sciences by the Medical Ethics Framework

1. See also Juritzen *et al.* (2011), Bartlett (2008), and McDonald (2000).
2. German Data Forum (RatSWD) (2016) offers detailed insights about developments in Germany with respect to research ethics and ethics review.
3. Given the disciplinary diversity of committee memberships, their varied training or backgrounds, and the size of universities, it is difficult to collect statistical data on ethics committees. Social comparisons among ethics committees are therefore meaningless.
4. See also Susan Boser (2007) for an excellent overview of the challenges that researchers face in ethics committees when doing participatory research.
5. The *New Brunswick Declaration* produced at the 2012 Ethics Rupture Summit held in Fredericton, New Brunswick, specifies the need for ethics committees to treat researchers with respect (van den Hoonaard and Tolich 2016).

*Notes*

6. We learn from Kevin Haggerty (2022) that a Quebec Superior Court decision in 2017 has granted a *de facto* form of "researcher exemption" in Canada that prevents prosecutors from being able to subpoena a researcher's notes.

## 4 | The Anthropological Stance in Ethical Research

1. I am indebted to Peter Pels of Leiden University, whose extensive writing on the history of ethics in anthropology formed the basis of this chapter.
2. See http://ethics.americananthro.org/category/statement/.

## 6 | Current Debates in the Research-Ethics Community

1. The National Research Council of the National Academies (2014) covers the text known as "the Common Rule" and its analysis. The American Anthropological Association provides a useful tool for ethics committees to consider the many fundamental ways that anthropological research differs from the prevailing ethics codes in the United States (see https://www.americananthro.org/ParticipateAndAdvocate/Content.aspx?ItemNumber=1652).
2. *Institutional Review Blog* (Schrag 2010a; 2012) carries a robust debate with an exchange of ideas by Stuart Nicholls *et al.* (2012), Adam Hedgecoe (2012), Sean Jennings (2012), and Tim Bond (2012). We must stop colluding with the current system of ethics regulation and call it by its proper name—a "creeping tyranny [that] feeds on our reasonableness" (Dingwall 2006:57). Ethical governance and professional ethics should not be confused. Ethical governance is about censorship and the exercise of power. Whatever the motives for which it is advanced, it is profoundly anti-democratic. Professional ethics is about respect for our common humanity and the mutual obligations that this creates. It is about integrity and virtue in our scholarship.
3. I wish to pay tribute to Jan Wong, well known in the field of journalism for her broad international experience, who often would deliberate with social scientists about the sense of ethics journalists accrue from their formal education and from handling newspaper and blog-related assignments.

## 7 | Towards a New Approach in the Social Sciences

1. Focusing on the thrust of these questions, I have deleted a few fragments from Weeks's email and paraphrased others.

## Appendix

1. This appendix was originally published as "The New Brunswick Declaration on Research Ethics, Integrity, and Governance" in the *Journal of Clinical Research & Bioethics*, March 31, 2016. DOI: 10.4172/2155-9627.1000268. © 2016 WC van den Hoonaard. This is an open-access article distributed under the terms of the Creative Commons Attribution License, which permits unrestricted use, distribution, and reproduction in any medium, provided the original author and source are credited. The original text has been lightly edited for this book.
2. More typically, it is the social science journals that carry articles related to the disgruntlements of social scientists with the ethics regime. It is important for journals like the *Journal of Clinical Research & Bioethics* to carry an article such as this one.
3. My own personal bibliography on ethics in social science research lists 330–350 articles. Medical researchers have also underscored the problematic nature of ethics regimes. See Whitney (2012), Edwards *et al.* (2004), Fistein and Quilligan (2012), Fost and Levine (2007), Garrard and Dawson (2005), Goldacre (2008), Jamrozik and Kolybaba (1999), van den Hoonaard (2002a; 2006b), Wynn (2016), and Minnis (2004). Upon request I will make this bibliography available to anyone so interested.
4. *American Ethnologist, Anthropology News, Canadian Social Work Review, Chronicle of Higher Education, Educational Researcher, IRB: Ethics & Human Research, Journal of Applied Communication Research, Journal of Empirical Research on Human Research Ethics, Qualitative Inquiry, Qualitative Research, Qualitative Sociology, Signs: Journal of Women in Culture and Society, Sociology*, and so on.
5. The *TCPS* 2 (Canadian Institutes of Health Research *et al.* 2014) explains that mandatory provisions are signalled by the use of the term "shall" whereas guidance for the interpretation of the core principles is generally indicated by use of the term "should." The whole *TCPS* 2 contains 298 "shalls," 514 "shoulds," and 121 "musts." Some of these provisions are cast as "research directives."
6. See http://www.hhs.gov/ohrp/humansubjects/guidance/45cfr46.html (Office for Human Research Protections 2008).
7. *The Ethics Rupture: Exploring Alternatives to Formal Research-Ethics Review* (van den Hoonaard and Hamilton, 2016), contains the presentations made at that summit.
8. For more detailed descriptions of the *New Brunswick Declaration*, see van den Hoonaard (2013a; 2013b; 2014b).
9. I still regularly hear claims by REB members that researchers are "lackadaisical," "slovenly," or "lazy" when it comes to conducting ethical research.

# References

Absolon, Kathleen E. 2011. *Kaandossiwin: How We Come to Know*. Halifax, NS: Fernwood Publishing.

Adams, Richard N. 1981. "Ethical Principles in Anthropological Research: One or Many?" *Human Organization* 40(2):155–60.

Akesson, Bree. 2018. "Every Corner Tells a Story: Using Neighbourhood Walks and GPS to Understand Children's Sense of Place." Pp. 232–36 in *The Craft of Qualitative Research: A Handbook*, edited by S.W. Kleinknecht, L-J.K. van den Scott, and C.B. Sanders. Toronto, ON: Canadian Scholars' Press.

Allegretti, Joseph. 1998. "A Religious Perspective on Legal Practice and Ethics." *Fordham Law Review* 66(4):1101–29.

American Anthropological Association. 2012. "Principles of Professional Responsibility." Retrieved January 8, 2023 (https://ethics.americananthro.org/category/statement/).

American Anthropological Association. 2016. "AAA Commentary on Proposed Changes to the Common Rule." Retrieved December 7, 2022. (https://www.americananthro.org/ParticipateAndAdvocate/AdvocacyDetail.aspx?ItemNumber=13302).

Anonymous. 2023. "Covenant." *Wikipedia: The Free Encyclopedia*. Retrieved January 12, 2023 (https://en.wikipedia.org/wiki/Covenant).

Athens, Lonnie. 2017. *Dominance and Subjugation in Everyday Life*. New York: Routledge.

Baez, Benjamin. 2002. "Confidentiality in Qualitative Research: Reflections on Secrets, Power and Agency." *Qualitative Research* 2:35–58.

Baggini, Julian. 2018. "How to Compare Fruit: The Limited Ambitions of Ethical Thinking." *Times Literary Supplement*, May 25, 7–9.

Barnes, John A. 1977. *The Ethics of Inquiry in Social Science: Three Lectures*. Oxford, UK: Oxford University Press.

Barnes, Kenneth J. 1976. "Freedom of Expression at Yale." *AAUP Bulletin* 62(1):28–42.

Barrett, Robert J. and Damon B. Parker. 2003. "Rites of Consent: Negotiating Research Participation in Diverse Cultures." *Monash Bioethics Review* 22:9–26.

Bartlett, Edward E. 2008. "International Analysis of Institutional Review Boards Registered with the U.S. Office for Human Research Protections." *Journal of Empirical Research on Human Research Ethics* 3(4):49–56.

Becker, Howard S. 1951. "The Professional Dance Musician and His Audience." *American Journal of Sociology* 57(2):136–44.

Becker, Howard S. 1963. *Outsiders: Studies in the Sociology of Deviance.* New York: Free Press.

Becker, Howard S. 2004. "Comment on Kevin D. Haggerty, 'Ethics Creep: Governing Social Science Research in the Name of Ethics.'" *Qualitative Sociology* 27(4):415–16.

Bell, Kirsten. 2014. "Resisting Commensurability: Against Informed Consent as an Anthropological Virtue." *American Anthropologist* 116(3):511–22.

Benbow, Sarah and Jodi Hall. 2018. "Negotiating Tensions in Exiting the Field of Critical Qualitative Research." Pp. 311–18 in *The Craft of Qualitative Research: A Handbook*, edited by S.W. Kleinknecht, L-J.K. van den Scott, and C.B. Sanders. Toronto, ON: Canadian Scholars' Press.

Benedict, Ruth. 1934. *Patterns of Culture.* Boston, MA: Houghton Mifflin.

Benedict, Ruth. 1946. *The Chrysanthemum and the Sword: Patterns of Japanese Culture.* Boston, MA: Houghton Mifflin.

Berkman, Benjamin E., David Wendler, Haley K. Sullivan, and Christine Grady. 2017. "A Proposed Process for Reliably Updating the Common Rule." *American Journal of Bioethics* 17(7):8–14.

Bhattacharya, Kakali. 2007. "Consenting to the Consent Form: What Are the Fixed and Fluid Understandings Between the Researcher and the Researched?" *Qualitative Inquiry* 13(8):1095–115.

Biswas, Subir. 2015. "Ethics in Anthropological Research: Responsibilities to Participants." *Human Biology Review* 4(3):250–63.

Bledsoe, Caroline H., Bruce Sherin, Adam G. Gallinsky, Nathalia M. Headley, Carol A. Heimer, Erik Kjeldgaard, James Lindgren, Jon D. Miller, Michael E. Roloff, and David H. Uttal. 2007. "Regulating Creativity: Research and Survival in the IRB Iron Cage." *Northwestern University Law Review* 101(2):593–641.

Blok, Anton. 1973. "A Note on Ethics and Power." *Human Organization* 32(1):95–98.

Bok, Sissela. 1999. *Lying: Moral Choice in Public and Private Life.* New York: Vintage.

Bond, Tim. 2012. "Ethical Imperialism or Ethical Mindfulness? Rethinking Ethical Review for Social Sciences." *Research Ethics* 8(2):97–112.

Boser, Susan. 2006. "Ethics and Power in Community–Campus Partnerships for Research." *Action Research* 4(1):9–21.

Boser, Susan. 2007. "Power, Ethics, and the IRB: Dissonance over Human Participant Review of Participatory Research." *Qualitative Inquiry* 13(8):1060–73.

Bosk, Charles L. 2007. "The New Bureaucracies of Virtue or When Form Fails to Follow Function." *Political and Legal Anthropology Review* 30(2):192–209.

Bosk, Charles L. and Raymond G. De Vries. 2004. "Bureaucracies of Mass Deception: Institutional Review Boards and the Ethics of Ethnographic Research." *Annals of the American Academy of Political and Social Science* 595(1):249–63.

Brassington, Iain. 2016. "The Function of—and Need for—Institutional Review Boards: Review of *The Censor's Hand: The Misregulation of Human-Subject Research*." *Pacific Standard* 9(2):68–69.

Breen, Kerry J. 2002. "Improving Australia's Ethical Review Processes: Slow and Steady Wins the Race." *Monash Bioethics Review* 21(3):S58–S62.

Brydon-Miller, Mary. 2009. "Covenantal Ethics and Action Research: Exploring a Common Foundation for Social Research." Pp. 243–58 in *The Handbook of Social Research Ethics*, edited by D. Mertens and P. Ginsberg. Los Angeles, CA: SAGE.

Brydon-Miller, Mary. 2011. "Ethical Principles, Ethical Practice: Community Covenantal Ethics as a Framework for Strengthening Ethical Practice in Action Research." Presentation given at Trinity College, Dublin, Ireland. July 14.

Brydon-Miller, Mary. 2013. "Community Covenantal Ethics and Structured Ethical Reflection: Enacting the Values of Action Research." Presentation given at Manchester Metropolitan University, Manchester, United Kingdom. February 20.

Buck, Christopher. 1998. "A Symbolic Profile of the Bahá'í Faith." *Journal of Bahá'í Studies* 8(4):1–48.

Buckle, Jennifer L., Sonya Corbin Dwyer, and Marlene Jackson. 2010. "Qualitative Bereavement Research: Incongruity Between the Perspectives of Participants and Research Ethics Boards." *International Journal of Social Research Methodology* 13(2):111–25.

Bull, Julie R. 2010. "Research with Aboriginal Peoples: Authentic Relationships as a Precursor to Ethical Research." *Journal of Empirical Research on Human Research Ethics* 5(4):3–22.

Bull, Julie R. 2019. "Relational and Reflective Research: People, Policies, and Priorities at Play in Ethically Approving Research with Indigenous Peoples." PhD dissertation, University of New Brunswick.

Burawoy, Michael. 2005. "For Public Sociology." *American Sociological Review* 70(1):4–28.

Burris, Scott C. 2008. "Regulatory Innovation in the Governance of Human Subjects Research: A Cautionary Tale and Some Modest Proposals." *Regulation & Governance* 2(1):65–84.

Burris, Scott and Jen Welsh. 2007. "Regulatory Paradox in the Protection of Human Research Subjects: A Review of OHRP Enforcement Letters." *Northwestern University Law Review* 101(2):643–85.

# References

Calvey, David. 2017. *Covert Research: The Art, Politics and Ethics of Undercover Fieldwork*. Thousand Oaks, CA: SAGE.

Canadian Institutes of Health Research (CIHR), Natural Sciences and Engineering Research Council of Canada (NSERC), and Social Sciences and Humanities Research Council (SSHRC). 2014. *Tri-Council Policy Statement: Ethical Conduct for Research Involving Humans* (TCPS). Ottawa, ON: Government of Canada Panel on Research Ethics.

Canadian Institutes of Health Research (CIHR), Natural Sciences and Engineering Research Council of Canada (NSERC), and Social Sciences and Humanities Research Council (SSHRC). 2018. *Tri-Council Policy Statement: Ethical Conduct for Research Involving Humans* (TCPS 2). Ottawa, ON: Government of Canada Panel on Research Ethics.

Cannella, Gaile S. 2004. "Regulatory Power: Can a Feminist Poststructuralist Engage in Research Oversight?" *Qualitative Inquiry* 10(2):235–45.

Carpenter, Dale. 2007. "Institutional Review Boards, Regulatory Incentives, and Some Modest Proposals for Reform." *Northwestern University Law Review* 101(2):687–705.

Carr, Caleb T. 2015. "Spotlight on Ethics: Institutional Review Boards as Systemic Bullies." *Journal of Higher Education Policy and Management* 37(1):14–29.

Castillo, Rosa Cordillera A. 2018. "Subverting 'Formalised' Ethics Through Mainstreaming Critical Research Ethics and a Responsive Review Process." *Social Anthropology* 26(3):406–07.

Childress, Herb. 2006. "The Anthropologist and the Crayons: Changing Our Focus from Avoiding Harm to Doing Good." *Journal of Empirical Research on Human Research Ethics* 1(2):79–88.

Christians, Clifford G. 2000. "Ethics and Politics in Qualitative Research." Pp. 139–64 in *Handbook of Qualitative Research*, 2nd ed., edited by N.K. Denzin and Y.S. Lincoln. London, UK: SAGE.

Clegg, Stewart R., David Courpasson, and Nelson Phillips. 2006. *Power and Organizations*. London, UK: SAGE.

Cline, Scott. 2012. "'Dust Clouds of Camels Shall Cover You': Covenant and the Archival Endeavor." *The American Archivist* 75(2):282–96.

Cloke, Paul, Phil Cooke, Jenny Cursons, Paul Milbourne, and Rebekah Widdowfield. 2000. "Ethics, Reflexivity and Research: Encounters with Homeless People." *Ethics, Place, and Environment* 3(2):133–54.

Coleman, Carl H. and Marie-Charlotte Bouësseau. 2008. "How Do We Know that Research Ethics Committees Are Really Working? The Neglected Role of Outcomes Assessment in Research Ethics Review." *BMC Medical Ethics* 9(6):1–7.

Collins, Randy. 1975. *Conflict Sociology: Toward an Explanatory Science.* Cambridge, MA: Academic Press.

Collins, Randy. 1988. *Theoretical Sociology.* San Diego, CA: Harcourt College Publishers.

Coomber, Ross. 2002. "'Signing Your Life Away?' Why Research Ethics Committees (REC) Shouldn't Always Require Written Confirmation that Participants in Research Have Been Informed of the Aims of the Study and Their Rights: The Case of Criminal Populations." *Sociological Research Online* 7(1):218–21.

Cooper, M.C. 1988. "Covenantal Relationships: Grounding for the Nursing Ethic." *Advances in Nursing Science* 10(4):48–59.

Corrigan, Oonagh. 2003. "Empty Ethics: The Problem with Informed Consent." *Sociology of Health and Illness* 25(7):768–92.

Costas, Jana, and Christopher Grey. 2014. "Bringing Secrecy into the Open: Towards a Theorization of the Social Processes of Organizational Secrecy." *Organization Studies* 35(10):1423–47.

Council of the European Union. 2015. "Draft Council Conclusions on Research Integrity." Retrieved January 9, 2023 (https://data.consilium.europa.eu/doc/document/ST-14201-2015-INIT/en/pdf).

Cressey, Paul. 1932. *The Taxi-Dance Hall: A Sociological Study in Commercialized Recreation and City Life.* Chicago, IL: University of Chicago Press.

Cross, Jennifer E., Kathleen Pickering, and Matthew Hickey. 2015. "Community-based Participatory Research Ethics, and Institutional Review Boards: Untying a Gordian Knot." *Critical Sociology* 41(7–8):1007–26.

Cutcliffe, John R. and Paul Ramcharan. 2002. "Leveling the Playing Field? Exploring the Merits of the Ethics-as-Process Approach for Judging Qualitative Research Proposals." *Qualitative Health Research* 12(7):1000–10.

Dalton, Melville. 1959. *Men Who Manage.* New York: John Wiley and Sons.

Davis, Fred. 1973. "The Martian and the Convert: Ontological Polarities in Social Research." *Urban Life and Culture* 2(3):333–43.

de Sola Pool, Ithiel, ed. 1977. *The Social Impact of the Telephone.* Cambridge, MA: MIT Press.

De Vries, Raymond, Debra A. DeBruin, and Andrew Goodgame. 2004. "Ethics Review of Social, Behavioral, and Economic Research: Where Should We Go from Here?" *Ethics and Behavior* 14(4):351–68.

Dillman, Caroline M. 1977. "Ethical Problems in Social Science Research Peculiar to Participant Observation." *Human Organization* 36(4):405–07.

Dingwall, Robert. 2006. "Confronting the Anti-Democrats: The Unethical Nature of Ethical Regulation in Social Science." *Medical Sociology Online* 1(1):51–58.

Dingwall, Robert. 2016. "The Social Costs of Ethics Regulation." Pp. 25–52 in *The Ethics Rupture: Exploring Alternatives to Formal Research-Ethics Review*, edited by W.C. van den Hoonaard and A. Hamilton. Toronto, ON: University of Toronto Press.

Dingwall, Robert, Ron Iphofen, Janet Lewis, John Oates, and Nathan Emmerich. 2017. "Towards Common Principles for Social Science Research Ethics: A Discussion Document for the Academy of Social Sciences." Pp. 111–23 in *Finding Common Ground: Consensus in Research Ethics Across the Social Sciences*, edited by R. Iphofen. Bingley, UK: Emerald Publishing.

Dobrin, Lise and Rena Lederman. 2011. "Comments on Proposed Changes to the Common Rule (76 FR 44512)." Report commissioned by the American Anthropological Association. Retrieved December 7, 2022 (http://s3.amazonaws.com/rdcms-aaa/files/production/public/Human-Subjects-Research-2011.pdf).

Dobrin, Lise and Rena Lederman. 2016. "Commentary on Notice of Proposed Rulemaking (80 FR 53933 published 09-08-2015; docket ID HHS–OPHS–2015–0008): Proposals for Modernizing the Common Rule." Report commissioned by the American Anthropological Association. Retrieved December 7, 2022 (https://s3.amazonaws.com/rdcms-aaa/files/production/public/AAACommentary_Common_Rule_NPRM_2016.pdf).

Dodds, Susan. 2002. "Is the Australian HREC System Sustainable?" *Monash Bioethics Review: Ethics Committee Supplement* 21(3):43–57.

Dougherty, Debbie S. and Michael W. Kramer. 2005. "A Rationale for Scholarly Examination of Institutional Review Boards: A Case Study." *Journal of Applied Communication Research* 33(3):183–88.

Douglas, Jack D. 1976. *Investigative Social Research: Individual and Team Field Research*. Thousand Oaks, CA: SAGE.

Douglas, Jack D., Paul K. Rasmussen, and Carol Ann Flanagan. 1977. *The Nude Beach* (Volume 1 of *Sociological Observations*). Beverly Hills. CA: SAGE.

Downie, Jocelyn. 2006. "The Canadian Agency for the Oversight of Research Involving Humans: A Reform Proposal." *Accountability in Research* 13(1):75–100.

Dziak, Kathleen, Roger Anderson, Mary Ann Sevick, Carol S. Weisman, Douglas W. Levine, and Sarah Hudson Scholle. 2005. "Variations Among Institutional Review Board Reviews in a Multisite Health Services Research Study." *Health Services Research* 40(1):279–90.

Eckenwiler, Lisa A., Dafna Feinholz, Carolyn Ells, and Toby Schonfeld. 2008. "The Declaration of Helsinki Through a Feminist Lens." *International Journal of Feminist Approaches to Bioethics* 1(1):161–77.

Edwards, Nichole. 2018. "On (Still) Being Emotionally Attached to the Field." Pp. 326–31 in *The Craft of Qualitative Research: A Handbook,* edited by S.W. Kleinknecht, L-J.K. van den Scott, and C.B. Sanders. Toronto, ON: Canadian Scholars' Press.

Edwards, Sarah J.L., Simon Kirchin, and Richard Huxtable. 2004. "Research Ethics Committees and Paternalism." *Journal of Medical Ethics* 30(1):88–91.

Ehrenreich, Barbara. 2010. *Nickel and Dimed: On (Not) Getting By in America.* New York: Metropolitan Books.

Ellis, Carolyn. 2007. "Telling Secrets, Revealing Lives: Relational Ethics in Research with Intimate Others." *Qualitative Inquiry* 13(1):3–29.

Emmerich, Nathan. 2016. "Reframing Research Ethics: Towards a Professional Ethics for the Social Sciences." *Sociological Research Online* 21(4):16–29.

EthNav 2018. "Amending the ASA Ethical Guidelines." ASA Ethical Guidelines Review Working Group (EGG). (https://www.theasa.org/ethics/ethnav.phtml).

Fanon, Frantz. 1963. *The Wretched of the Earth.* New York: Grove Weidenfeld.

Feldman, Shelley and Linda Shaw. 2018. "The Epistemological and Ethical Challenges of Archiving and Sharing Qualitative Data." *American Behavioral Scientist* 63(6):699–721.

Fine, Gary Alan. 1996. *Kitchens: The Culture of Restaurant Work.* Berkeley, CA: University of California Press.

Fine, Gary Alan. 2019. "Relational Distance and Epistemic Generosity: The Power of Detachment in Skeptical Ethnography." *Sociological Methods & Research* 48(4):828–49.

Fistein, Elizabeth and Sally Quilligan. 2012. "In the Lion's Den? Experiences of Interaction with Research Ethics Committees." *Journal of Medical Ethics* 38(4):224–27.

Fitzgerald, Maureen and Elisa Yule. 2004. "Open and Closed Committees." *Monash Bioethics Review: Ethics Committee Supplement* 23(2):35–49.

Fleming, Michael A. 2018. "Researching Truck Drivers: Difficult Data Collection and Proving Oneself Amidst a Culture of Suspicious Masculinity." Pp. 92–97 in *The Craft of Qualitative Research: A Handbook,* edited by S.W. Kleinknecht, L-J.K. van den Scott, and C.B. Sanders. Toronto, ON: Canadian Scholars' Press.

Fost, Norman and Robert J. Levine. 2007. "The Dysregulation of Human Subjects Research." *JAMA* 298(18):2196–98.

Fowler, Marsha D. 2017. "Why the History of Nursing Ethics Matters." *Nursing Ethics* 24(3):292–304.

Fraser, Malcolm. 2014. "It's Time to Define a Covenant of Human Ethics." *The Guardian*, April 1. Retrieved January 23, 2023 (https://www.theguardian.com/commentisfree/2014/apr/01/its-time-to-define-a-covenant-of-human-ethics).

Galliher, John F. 1980. "Social Scientists' Ethical Responsibilities to Superordinates: Looking Upward Meekly." *Social Problems* 27(3):298–308.

Galliher, John F., Wayne Brekhus, and David P. Keys. 2006. *Laud Humphreys: Prophet of Homosexuality and Sociology*. Madison, WI: University of Wisconsin Press.

Garrard, Eve and Andrew Dawson. 2005. "What Is the Role of the Research Ethics Committee? Paternalism, Inducement, and Harm in Research Ethics." *Journal of Medical Ethics* 31(7):419–23.

German Data Forum (RatSWD). 2016. *Ethical Principles and Review Procedures in Social and Economic Research*. Report of the German Data Forum's Working Group on Research Ethics, December 5.

Giddens, Anthony. 1991. *Introduction to Sociology*. New York: W.W. Norton.

Goffman, Erving. 1959. *The Presentation of Self in Everyday Life*. New York: Doubleday.

Goffman, Erving. 1961. *Asylums: Essays on the Social Situation of Mental Patients and Other Inmates*. New York: Doubleday.

Goffman, Erving. 1972. *Relations in Public: Microstudies of the Public Order*. New York: Penguin.

Goldacre, Ben. 2008. "Ticking the Boxes Before Trying to Save Lives," *The Guardian*, February 23. Retrieved December 7, 2022 (https://www.theguardian.com/science/2008/feb/23/badscience.medicalresearch).

Gontcharov, Ivor. 2013. "Methodological Crisis in the Social Sciences: The New Brunswick Declaration as a New Paradigm in Research Ethics Governance?" *Transnational Legal Theory* 4(1):146–56.

Gordon, Judith B., Robert J. Levine, Carolyn M. Mazure, Philip E. Rubin, Barry R. Schaller, and John L. Young. 2011. "Social Contexts Influence Ethical Considerations of Research." *American Journal of Bioethics* 11(5):24–30.

Grayson, J. Paul and Richard Myles. 2005. "How Research Ethics Boards Are Undermining Survey Research on Canadian University Students." *Journal of Academic Ethics* 2(4):293–314.

Gunsalus, C. Kristina. 2003. "Human Subject Protections: Some Thoughts on Costs and Benefits in the Humanistic Disciplines." Illinois Public Law Research Paper No. 03-02.

Gunsalus, C. Kristina, Edward M. Bruner, Nicholas C. Burbules, Leon Dash, Matthew Finkin, Joseph P. Goldberg, William T. Greenough, Gregory A. Miller, Michael G. Pratt, Masumi Iriye, and Deb Aronson. 2007. "The Illinois White Paper: Improving the System for Protecting Human Subjects: Counteracting IRB 'Mission Creep.'" *Qualitative Inquiry* 13(5):617–49.

Gunther, Katja M. 2009. "The Politics of Names: Rethinking the Methodological and Ethical Significance of Naming People, Organizations, and Places." *Qualitative Research* 9(4):411–21.

Haggerty, Kevin D. 2004. "Ethics Creep: Governing Social Science Research in the Name of Ethics." *Qualitative Sociology* 27(4):391–414.

Haggerty, Kevin D. 2022. "Uneasy Relations: Crime Ethnographies and Research Ethics." In *The Oxford Handbook of Ethnographies of Crime and Criminal Justice*, edited by S.M. Bucerius, K.D. Haggerty, and L. Berardi. Oxford, UK: Oxford University Press.

Hamilton, Ann. 2002. "Institutional Review Boards: Politics, Power, Purpose and Process in a Regulatory Organization." PhD dissertation, University of Oklahoma.

Hammersley, Martyn and Anna Traianou. 2012. *Ethics in Qualitative Research: Controversies and Contexts*. London, UK: SAGE.

Hedgecoe, Adam M. 2012. "Trust and Regulatory Organizations: The Role of Local Knowledge and Facework in Research Ethics Review." *Social Studies of Science* 42(5):662–83.

Hedgecoe, Adam M. 2016. "Reputational Risk, Academic Freedom and Research Ethics Review." *Sociology* 50(3):486–501.

Helgeland, Ingeborg Marie. 2005. "'Catch 22' of ResearchEthics: Ethical Dilemmas in Follow-up Studies of Marginal Groups." *Qualitative Inquiry* 11(4):549–69.

Hillier, Cathlene and Emily Milne. 2018. "You're an Alien to Us: Autoethnographic Accounts of Two Researchers' Experiences in an Organizational Setting." Pp. 98–104 in *The Craft of Qualitative Research: A Handbook*, edited by S.W. Kleinknecht, L-J.K. van den Scott, and C.B. Sanders. Toronto, ON: Canadian Scholars' Press.

Hilsen, Anne Inga. 2006. "And They Shall Be Known By Their Deeds: Ethics and Politics in Action Research." *Action Research* 4(1):23–36.

Hilsen, Anne Inga and Tove Helvik. 2014. "The Construction of Self in Social Medias, Such as Facebook." *AI & Society* 29(1):3–10.

Hilton, Timothy P., Peter R. Fawson, Thomas Sullivan, and Cornell R. DeJong. 2019. *Applied Social Research: A Tool for the Human Services*. 10th ed. New York: Springer.

Holmwood, John. 2010. "Sociology's Misfortune: Disciplines, Interdisciplinarity and the Impact of Audit Culture." *British Journal of Sociology* 61(4):639–58.

Hudson, Maui L. and Khyla Russell. 2009. "The Treaty of Waitangi and Research Ethics in Aotearoa." *Journal of Bioethical Inquiry* 6(1):61–68.

Hughes, Everett C. 1971. *The Sociological Eye: Selected Papers*. Piscataway, NJ: Transaction.

# References

Humphreys, Laud. 1970. *Tearoom Trade: Impersonal Sex in Public Places*. Piscataway, NJ: Transaction.

Humphreys, Stephen, Hilary Thomas, and Robyn Martin. 2014. "Medical Dominance Within Research Ethics Committees." *Policies and Quality Assurance* 21(6):366–88.

Husain, Abbar R. 2018. "A Reflection on Challenges and Negotiation in the Context of International Fieldwork." Pp. 207–17 in *The Craft of Qualitative Research: A Handbook*, edited by S.W. Kleinknecht, L-J.K. van den Scott, and C.B. Sanders. Toronto, ON: Canadian Scholars' Press.

Inckle, Kay. 2015. "Promises, Promises: Lessons in Research Ethics from the Belfast Project and 'The Rape Tape' Case." *Sociological Research Online* 20(1):59–71.

Israel, Mark. 2015. *Research Ethics and Integrity for Social Scientists*. 2nd ed. London, UK: SAGE.

Israel, Mark. 2017. "Ethical imperialism? Exporting Research Ethics to the Global South." Pp. 89–102 in *The SAGE Handbook of Qualitative Research Ethics*, edited by R. Iphofen and M. Tolich. Thousand Oaks, CA: SAGE.

Jamrozik, Konrad and Marlene Kolybaba. 1999. "Are Ethics Committees Retarding the Improvement of Health Services in Australia?" *Medical Journal of Australia* 170(1):26–28.

Jansen II, William H. 1973. "The Applied Man's Burden: The Problem of Ethics and Applied Anthropology." *Human Organization* 32(3):325–29.

Jennings, Sean. 2012. "Response to Schrag: What Are Ethics Committees for Anyway? A Defence of Social Science Research Ethics Review." *Research Justice* 8(2):87–96.

Johnson, John M. 1975. *Doing Field Research*. New York: Free Press.

Johnston, Matthew S. 2018. "Politics and Tensions of Doing Transgender Research: Lessons Learned by a Straight-White-Cisgender Man." Pp. 85–91 in *The Craft of Qualitative Research: A Handbook,* edited by S.W. Kleinknecht, L-J.K. van den Scott, and C.B. Sanders. Toronto, ON: Canadian Scholars' Press.

Juritzen, Truls I., Harald Gromen, and Kristin Heggen. 2011. "Protecting Vulnerable Research Participants: A Foucault-inspired Analysis of Ethics Committees." *Nursing Ethics* 18(5):640–50.

King, Nancy M.P., Gail Henderson, and Jane Stein. 1999. *Beyond Regulations: Ethics in Human Subject Research*. Chapel Hill, NC: University of North Carolina Press.

Kleinknecht, Steven. 2018. "Personal Reputation as an 'In' to Field Research Settings." Pp. 121–26 in *The Craft of Qualitative Research: A Handbook,* edited by S.W. Kleinknecht, L-J.K. van den Scott, and C.B. Sanders. Toronto, ON: Canadian Scholars' Press.

Kleinknecht, Steven, Lisa-Jo K. van den Scott, and Carrie B. Sanders, eds. 2018. *The Craft of Qualitative Research: A Handbook*. Toronto, ON: Canadian Scholars' Press.

Kohn, Tamara and Cris Shore. 2017. "The Ethics of University Ethics Committees: Risk Management and the Research Imagination." Pp. 229–50 in *Death of the Public University? Uncertain Futures for Higher Education in the Knowledge Economy*, edited by S. Wright and C. Shore. New York: Berghahn Books.

Kondro, Wayne. 2016. "Canadian Researcher in Legal Battle to Keep Her Interviews Confidential." *Science*, November 22. Retrieved December 7, 2022 (https://www.science.org/content/article/canadian-researcher-legal-battle-keep-her-interviews-confidential).

Landry, Deborah. 2018. "Listening to Streets and Watching Paint Dry: Collecting Other Forms of Data." Pp. 218–24 in *The Craft of Qualitative Research: A Handbook*, edited by S.W. Kleinknecht, L-J.K. van den Scott, and C.B. Sanders. Toronto, ON: Canadian Scholars' Press.

Langlois, Anthony J. 2011. "Political Research and Human Research Ethics Committees." *Australian Journal of Political Science* 46(1):141–56.

Lederman, Doug. 2011. "Updating the Common Rule." *Inside Higher Ed*, August 3. Retrieved December 7, 2022 (https://www.insidehighered.com/news/2011/08/03/updating-common-rule).

Lederman, Rena S. 2007. "Comparative Research: A Modest Proposal Concerning the Object of Ethics Regulation." *Political and Legal Anthropology Review* 30(2):305–27.

Lederman, Rena S. 2018. "Doing Anthropology Ethically Takes Practice: A US Perspective on Formalization." *Social Anthropology* 26(3):408–09.

Lee, Raymond M. and Claire M. Renzetti. 1990. "The Problems of Researching Sensitive Topics: An Overview and Introduction." *American Behavioral Scientist* 33(5):510–28.

Lofland, John F. and Robert A. Lejeune. 1960. "Initial Interaction of Newcomers in Alcoholics Anonymous: A Field Experiment in Class Symbols and Socialization." *Social Problems* 8(2):102–11.

Lotich, Patricia. 2022. "Nine Areas Your Organization Should Be Auditing." *The Thriving Small Business*, March 2. Retrieved December 7, 2022 (https://thethrivingsmallbusiness.com/internal-audit-process-2/).

Macionis, John J., Juanne Nancarrow Clarke, and Linda M. Gerber. 1994. *Sociology: Canadian Edition*. Scarborough, ON: Prentice-Hall.

Maiter, Sarah, Laura Simich, Nora Jacobson, and Julie Wise. 2008. "Reciprocity: An Ethic for Community-based Participatory Action Research." *Action Research* 6(3):305–25.

# References

Mannay, Dawn. 2018. "Ethnography in Inaccessible Fields: Drawing on Visual Approaches to Understand the Private Space of the Home." Pp. 237–44 in *The Craft of Qualitative Research: A Handbook*, edited by S.W. Kleinknecht, L-J.K. van den Scott, and C.B. Sanders. Toronto, ON: Canadian Scholars' Press.

Marlowe, Jay and Martin Tolich. 2015. "Shifting from Research Governance to Research Ethics: A Novel Paradigm for Ethical Review in Community-based Research." *Research Ethics* 11(4):178–91.

Martin, Debbie H. 2012. "Two-Eyed Seeing: A Framework for Understanding Indigenous and Non-Indigenous Approaches to Indigenous Health Research." *Canadian Journal of Nursing Research* 44(2):20–42.

Marzano, Marco. 2012. "Informed Consent." Pp. 443–56 in *The SAGE Handbook of Interview Research: The Complexity of the Craft*, edited by J.F. Gubrium, J.A. Holstein, A.B. Marvasti, and K.D. McKinney. Thousand Oaks, CA: SAGE.

Matheson, Donald. 2018. "An Exception to the Rule: Journalism and Research Ethics." Pp. 1–10 in *The SAGE Handbook of Qualitative Research Ethics*, edited by R. Iphofen and M. Tolich. Thousand Oaks, CA: SAGE.

Mayo, Elton. 1933. *The Human Problems of an Industrial Civilization*. New York: Macmillan.

McDonald, Michael. 2000. "The Governance of Health Research Involving Human Subjects (HRIHS)." Ottawa, ON: Law Commission of Canada.

McWilliams, Rita, Carl W. Hebden, and Adele M.K. Gilpin. 2006. "A Concept Paper: A Virtual Centralized IRB System." *Accountability in Research* 13(1):25–45.

Mead, Margaret, Eliot D. Chapple, and G. Gordon Brown. 1949. "Report of the Committee on Ethics." *Human Organization* 8(2):20–21.

Méndez, Mariza. 2013. "Autoethnography as a Research Method: Advantages, Limitations, and Criticisms." *Colombian Applied Linguistics Journal* 15(2):279–87.

Milgram, Stanley. 1974. *Obedience to Authority: An Experimental View*. New York: Harper.

Miller, Tina, Maxine Birch, Melanie Mauthner, and Julie Jessop, eds. 2002. *Ethics in Qualitative Research*. London, UK: SAGE.

Minnis, Helen J. 2004. "Ethics Review in Research: Ethics Committees Are Risk Averse." *BMJ* 328:710–11.

Mitchell, Richard G. 1993. *Secrecy and Fieldwork*. Newbury Park, CA: SAGE.

Moghimi, Seyed Mohammad. 2019. *Organizational Behavior Management: An Islamic Approach*. Bingley, UK: Emerald Publishing.

Moore, Carla. 2015. "Implementing Chapter 9 of the Tri-Council Policy Statement on the Ethics of Research Involving Aboriginal Peoples in Canada: How's That Going?" PhD dissertation, Dalhousie University.

National Research Council of the National Academies. 2014. "Proposed Revisions to the Common Rule for the Protection of Human Subjects in the Behavioral and Social Sciences." Washington, DC: National Academies Press.

New Zealand Ministry of Health. 2012. "Health and Disability Ethics Committees." Retrieved January 9, 2023 (https://ethics.health.govt.nz).

Nicholls, Stuart, Jamie Brehaut, and Raphael Saginur. 2012. "Social Science and Ethics Review: A Question of Practice Not Principle." *Research Ethics* 8(2):71–78.

Oakes, J. Michael. 2002. "Risks and Wrongs in Social Science Research: An Evaluator's Guide to the IRB." *Evaluation Research* 26(5):443–79.

Oakley, Ann. 2016. "Interviewing Women Again: Power, Time and the Gift." *Sociology* 50(1):195–213.

Office for Human Research Protections (OHRP). 2008. "Federal Policy for the Protection of Human Subjects, DHHS 45 CFR 46: International Compilation of Human Research Protections." Washington, DC: US Department of Health and Human Services.

O'Neill, Patrick. 2016. "Assessing Risk in Psychological Research." Pp. 119–32 in *The Ethics Rupture: Exploring Alternatives to Formal Research-Ethics Review*, edited by W.C. van den Hoonaard and A. Hamilton. Toronto, ON: University of Toronto Press.

Palys, Ted and John Lowman. 2010. "Going Boldly Where No One Has Gone Before? How Confidentiality Risk Aversion Is Killing Research on Sensitive Topics." *Journal of Academic Ethics* 8(4):265–84.

Panigrahi, Shrikant, Mohd Ridzuan Darun, Muhammad Waris A. Khan, and Senthil Kumar. 2017. "Promoting Research Governance Through Integrity and Ethical Practices: A Qualitative Study." Presentation given at the FGIC 1st Conference on Governance and Integrity, Yayasan Pahang, Kuantan, Malaysia. 3–4 April.

Parry, Odette and Natasha Mauthner. 2004. "Whose Data Are They Anyway? Practical, Legal, and Ethical Issues in Archiving Qualitative Research Data." *Sociology* 38(1):139–52.

Pels, Peter. 1999. "Professions of Duplexity: A Prehistory of Ethical Codes in Anthropology." *Current Anthropology* 40(2):101–36.

Pels, Peter. 2018a. "Data Management in Anthropology: The Next Phase in Ethics Governance?" *Social Anthropology* 26(3):391–96.

Pels, Peter. 2018b. "Response." *Social Anthropology* 26(3):411–12.

Pels, Peter, and Oscar Salemink. 1994. "Introduction: Five Theses on Ethnography as Colonial Practice." *History and Anthropology* 8(1–4):1–34.

Perez, Teresa Sandra. 2017. "In Support of Situated Ethics: Ways of Building Trust with Stigmatized Waste Pickers in Cape Town." *Qualitative Research* 19(2):148–63.

Poole, Roger. 1972. *Towards Deep Subjectivity*. New York: Harper Torch Books.

Posel, Deborah and Fiona C. Ross. 2014. "Opening up the Quandaries of Research Ethics: Beyond the Formalities of Institutional Review." Pp. 2–6 in *Ethical Quandaries in Social Research*, edited by D. Posel and F.C. Ross. Cape Town, South Africa: HSRC Press.

Power, Michael. 1999. *The Audit Society: Rituals of Verification*. Oxford, UK: Oxford University Press.

Pratt, Mary Louise. 1985. "Scratches on the Face of the Country; Or, What Mr. Barrow Saw in the Land of the Bushmen." *Critical Inquiry* 12(1):119–43.

Rashkover, Randi. 2017. "Covenantal Ethics and the 2016 Election." *Political Theology* 18(3):201–05.

Reynolds, Don. 2000. "Protecting the Human Subjects of Social Science Research: The Role of Institutional Review Boards." *Bioethics Forum* 16(4):31–36.

Riddell, Julia K., Salamanca, Angela, Pepler, Debra J., Cardinal, Shelley, & McIvor, Onowa. 2017. "Laying the Groundwork: A Practical Guide for Ethical Research with Indigenous Communities. *International Indigenous Policy Journal* 8(2):1-20.

Roberts, Lynne and David Indermaur. 2003. "Signed Consent Forms in Criminological Research: Protection for Researchers and Ethics Committees but a Threat to Research Participants?" *Psychiatry, Psychology and the Law* 10(2):289–99.

Robinson, Perry. 2019. "Relationships." *We Are Navajo*. (https://www.wearenavajo.org/healthy-living/relationships).

Roger, Kerstin and Javier Mignone. 2018. "Living Your Ethics: It's Not Just a Dusty Document." Pp. 46–52 in *The Craft of Qualitative Research: A Handbook*, edited by S.W. Kleinknecht, L-J.K. van den Scott, and C.B. Sanders. Toronto, ON: Canadian Scholars' Press.

Rose, Joanna and Annika Nilsson. 1999. "Sweden Considers More Oversight of Research." *Science* 283(5409):1829.

Rosenhan, David L. 1973. "On Being Sane in Insane Places." *Science* 179(4070):250–58.

Roth, Wolff-Michael. 2018. "Toward a Post-Constructivist Approach to Research Ethics." *Pedagogy: An International Journal* 8(2):103–25.

Roy, Donald. 1952. "Quota Restriction and Goldbricking in a Machine Shop." *American Journal of Sociology* 57(5):427–42.

Roy, Donald. 1959. "Banana Time: Job Satisfaction and Informal Interaction." *Human Organization* 18(4):158–68.

Russell, Cherry. 1999. "Interviewing Vulnerable Old People: Ethical and Methodological Implications of Imagining Our Subjects." *Journal of Aging Studies* 13(4):403–17.

Rusthoven, James J. 2014. *Covenantal Biomedical Ethics for Contemporary Medicine: An Alternative to Principles-based Ethics*. Eugene, OR: Pickwick Publications.

Saviano, Roberto. 2007. *Gomorrah*. New York: Farrar, Straus and Giroux.
Scarce, Rik. 1994. "(No) Trial (But) Tribulations: When Courts and Ethnography Conflict." *Journal of Contemporary Ethnography* 23(2):123–49.
Scarce, Rik. 1995. "Scholarly Ethics and Courtroom Antics: Where Researchers Stand in the Eye of the Law." *American Sociologist* 26(1):87–112.
Scarth, Bonnie. 2016. "Bereaved Participants' Reasons for Wanting Their Real Names Used in Thanatology Research." *Research Ethics* 12(2):80–96.
Scheper-Hughes, Nancy. 2004. "Parts Unknown: Undercover Ethnography of the Organs Trafficking Underworld." *Ethnography* 5(1):29–73.
Schimmel, Annemarie. 1994. *Deciphering the Signs of God: A Phenomenological Approach to Islam*. Albany, NY: State University of New York Press.
Schneider, Carl E. 2015. *The Censor's Hand: The Misregulation of Human-Subject Research*. Cambridge, MA: MIT Press.
Schrag, Zachary M. 2010a. "Smithsonian Frees Oral History, Journalism, and Folklore." *Institutional Review Blog*, July 30. Retrieved December 8, 2022 (http://www.institutionalreviewblog.com/2010/07/smithsonian-frees-oral-history.html).
Schrag, Zachary M. 2010b. *Ethical Imperialism: Institutional Review Boards and the Social Sciences, 1965–2009*. Baltimore, MD: Johns Hopkins University Press.
Schrag, Zachary M. 2011. "The Case Against Ethics Review in the Social Sciences." *Research Ethics* 7(4):120–31.
Schrag Zachary M. 2012. "What Is This Thing Called Research?" Retrieved from SSRN December 8, 2022 (http://papers.ssrn.com/sol3/papers.cfm?abstract_id=2182297).
Selinger, Suzanne. 1998. *Charlotte Von Kirschbaum and Karl Barth: A Study in Biography and the History of Theology*. University Park, PA: Penn State University Press.
Shaul, Randi Zlotnik. 2002. "Reviewing the Reviewers: The Vague Accountability of Research Ethics Committees." *Critical Care* 6(2):121–22.
Shulman, David. 1994. "Dirty Data and Investigative Methods: Some Lessons from Private Detective Work." *Journal of Contemporary Ethnography* 23(2):214–53.
Shore, Nancy. 2006. "Re-Conceptualizing the Belmont Report." *Journal of Community Practice* 14(4):5–26.
Shweder, Richard A. and Richard E. Nisbett. 2017. "Long-Sought Research Deregulation Is Upon Us: Don't Squander the Moment." *The Chronicle of Higher Education*, March 12. Retrieved November 2, 2022 (https://www.chronicle.com/article/long-sought-research-deregulation-is-upon-us-dont-squander-the-moment/).
Sieber, Joan E. and Martin Tolich. 2013. *Planning Ethically Responsible Research*. 2nd ed. Thousand Oaks, CA: SAGE.

# References

Simmel, Georg. 1906. "The Sociology of Secrecy and of Secret Societies." *American Journal of Sociology* 11(4):441–98.

Sium, Aman and Eric Ritskes. 2013. "Speaking Truth to Power: Indigenous Storytelling as an Act of Living Resistance." *Decolonization: Indigeneity, Education & Society* 2(1):i–x.

Smith, Linda Tuhiwai.. 1999. *Decolonizing Methodologies: Research and Indigenous Peoples*. New York: Zed Books.

Society for Applied Anthropology. 1951. "Ethics in Applied Anthropology." *Human Organization* 10(2):4.

Solnit, Rebecca. 2009. *A Paradise Built in Hell: The Extraordinary Communities that Arise in Disaster*. New York: Penguin Random House.

Srivastava, Sanjay. 2011. "CITI Is Still Misrepresenting Milgram's Obedience Research." *The Hardest Science*, July 6. Retrieved November 2, 2022 (https://thehardestscience.com/2011/07/06/citi-is-still-misrepresenting-milgrams-obedience-research/).

Stark, Laura M. 2011. *Behind Closed Doors: IRBs and the Making of Ethical Research*. Chicago, IL: University of Chicago Press.

Strathern, Marilyn. 2000. "New Accountabilities: Anthropological Studies in Audit, Ethics and the Academy." Pp. 1–18 in *Audit Cultures: Anthropological Studies in Accountability, Ethics and the Academy*, edited by M. Strathern. London, UK: Routledge.

Taylor, Alison, Robin Taylor-Neu, and Shauna Butterwick. 2018. "'Trying to Square the Circle': Research Ethics and Canadian Higher Education." *European Educational Research Journal* 19(1):56–71.

Tilley, Elizabeth and Kate Woodthorpe. 2011. "Is It the End for Anonymity as We Know It? A Critical Examination of the Ethical Principle of Anonymity in the Context of Twenty-first Century Demands on the Qualitative Researcher." *Qualitative Research* 11(2):197–212.

Traianou, Anna. 2018. "Ethical Regulation of Social Research Versus the Cultivation of Phrónēsis." Pp. 163–77 in *Virtue Ethics in the Conduct and Governance of Social Science Research*, edited by N. Emmerich. Bingley, UK: Emerald Publishing.

Truman, Carole. 2003. "Ethics and the Ruling Relations of Research Production." *Sociological Research Online* 8(1):70–80.

Truth and Reconciliation Commission of Canada (TRC). 2015. *Calls to Action*. Winnipeg, MB: Truth and Reconciliation Commission of Canada.

Tuck, Eve and K. Wayne Yang. 2012. "Decolonization Is Not a Metaphor." *Decolonization: Indigeneity, Education & Society* 1(1):1–40.

Turnbull, Colin. 1987. *The Mountain People*. New York: Simon & Schuster.

United States Department of Education. 2002. *Scientific Research in Education*. Washington, DC: National Academies Press.

University of Edinburgh. 2021. "Edinburgh Research Office." Retrieved January 7, 2023 (https://www.ed.ac.uk/research-office).

Vainio, Annukka. 2012. "Beyond Research Ethics: Anonymity as 'Ontology', 'Analysis' and 'Independence" *Qualitative Research* 13(6):685–98.

van den Hoonaard, Deborah K. 2001. *The Widowed Self: The Older Woman's Journey Through Widowhood*. Waterloo, ON: Wilfrid Laurier University Press.

van den Hoonaard, Deborah K. 2005. "Am I Doing It Right? Older Widows as Interview Participants in Qualitative Research." *Journal of Aging Studies* 19(3):393–406.

van den Hoonaard, Deborah K. 2018. *Qualitative Research in Action: A Canadian Primer*. 3rd ed. Toronto, ON: Oxford University Press.

van den Hoonaard, Deborah K. 2019. "Learning to Be Old: How Qualitative Research Contributes to Our Understanding of Ageism." *International Journal of Qualitative Methods* 17(1):1–8.

van den Hoonaard, Deborah K. and Will C. van den Hoonaard. 2021. "Ethics in Symbolic Interactionist Research." Pp. 391–99 in *The Routledge International Handbook of Symbolic Interactionism*, edited by D. vom Lehn, N. Ruiz-Junco, and W. Gibson. London, UK: Routledge.

van den Hoonaard, Will C. 1972. "Local-level Autonomy: A Case Study of an Icelandic Fishing Community." MA thesis, Department of Sociology, Memorial University of Newfoundland.

van den Hoonaard, Will C. 1991. *Silent Ethnicity: The Dutch of New Brunswick*. Fredericton, NB: New Ireland Press.

van den Hoonaard, Will C. 1996. *The Origins of the Bahá'í Community of Canada, 1898–1948*. Waterloo, ON: Wilfrid Laurier University Press.

van den Hoonaard, Will C. 2001. "Is Research-Ethics Review a Moral Panic?" *Canadian Review of Sociology and Anthropology* 38(1):19–36.

van den Hoonaard, Will C., ed. 2002. *Walking the Tightrope: Ethical Issues for Qualitative Researchers*. Toronto, ON: University of Toronto Press.

van den Hoonaard, Will C. 2003. "Current Developments in Research Ethics." Presentation given at St. Francis Xavier University, Antigonish, NS. May 30.

van den Hoonaard, Will C. 2004a. "The Ethics Trapeze: Is Ethics Review Changing the Social Sciences" Presentation given at InterArts Lecture Series, University of New Brunswick, Fredericton, NB. February 20.

# References

van den Hoonaard, Will C. 2004b. "Problems and Perspectives from Specific Disciplines." Presentation given at the Social and Behavioural Sciences and Humanities Ethics Conference, National Council on Ethical Human Research, University of Alberta, Edmonton, AB. February 22.

van den Hoonaard, Will C. 2005. "New Perspectives in Ethics and Public Health Research." Transdisciplinary training program in public health, population health and in health services and policy research. Canadian Institutes of Health Research Strategic Training Initiative and the Quebec Population Health Research Network, Montreal, QC. May 30.

van den Hoonaard, Will C. 2006a. "New Angles, Tangles, and Fads in the Ethics Review of Research." *Journal of Academic Ethics* 4(1–4):261–74.

van den Hoonaard, Will C. 2006b. "The Ethics Trapeze." *The Journal of Academic Ethics* 4(1–4):1–10.

van den Hoonaard, Will C. 2011. *The Seduction of Ethics: Transforming the Social Sciences*. Toronto, ON: University of Toronto Press.

van den Hoonaard, Will C. 2013a. "The Social and Policy Contexts of the New Brunswick Declaration on Research Ethics, Integrity, and Governance: A Commentary." *Journal of Empirical Research on Human Research Ethics* 8(2):104–09.

van den Hoonaard, Will C. 2013b. "Are We Asked to 'Other' Ourselves in a System with Social Scientists and the Research-Ethics Review Process?" Pp. 61–75 in *Finding Common Ground: Consensus in Research Ethics Across the Social Sciences*, edited by R. Iphofen. Bingley, UK: Emerald Publishing.

van den Hoonaard, Will C. 2013c. *Map Worlds: A History of Women in Cartography*. Waterloo, ON: Wilfrid Laurier University Press.

van den Hoonaard, Will C. 2013d. "The 'Ethics Rupture' Summit, Fredericton, New Brunswick, October 25–28, 2012." *Journal of Empirical Research on Human Research Ethics* 8(1):2–7.

van den Hoonaard, Will C. 2014a. "How Positivism Is Colonizing Qualitative Research Through Ethics Review." Pp. 173–94 in *Demarginalizing Voices: Commitment, Emotion, and Action in Qualitative Research*, edited by J.M. Kilty, S.C. Fabian, M. Felices-Luna. Vancouver, BC: University of British Columbia Press.

van den Hoonaard, Will C. 2014b. "The New Brunswick Declaration of Research Ethics: A Simple and Radical Perspective." *Canadian Journal of Sociology* 39(1):87–98.

van den Hoonaard, Will C. 2018. "The Vulnerability of Vulnerability: Why Social Science Researchers Should Abandon the Doctrine of Vulnerability." Pp. 305–21 in *Handbook of Research Ethics and Scientific Integrity*, edited by R. Iphofen. New York: Springer.

van den Hoonaard, Will C. and Anita Connolly. 2006. "Anthropological Research in Light of Research-Ethics Review: Canadian Master's Theses, 1995–2004." *Journal of Empirical Research on Human Research Ethics* 1(2):59–70.

van den Hoonaard, Will C. and Ann Hamilton, eds. 2016. *The Ethics Rupture: Exploring Alternatives to Formal Research-Ethics Review.* Toronto, ON: University of Toronto Press.

van den Hoonaard, Will C. and Martin Tolich. 2016. "The Making(s) of a Qualitative Code of Ethics: the Tri-Council Policy Statement: Ethical Conduct for Research Involving Humans." Pp. 59–68 in *Qualitative Research Ethics in Practice*, edited by M. Tolich. Walnut Creek, CA: Left Coast Press.

van den Scott, Lisa-Jo Kestin, 2016. "The Socialization of Contemporary Students by Ethics Boards: Malaise and Ethics for Graduate Students." Pp. 230–47 in *The Ethics Rupture: Exploring Alternatives to Formal Research-Ethics Review*, edited by W.C. van den Hoonaard and A. Hamilton. Toronto, ON: University of Toronto Press.

van den Scott, Lisa-Jo. 2018. "Section IV: Experiencing Emotions While Establishing Trust and Rapport." Pp. 105–06 in *The Craft of Qualitative Research: A Handbook*, edited by S.W. Kleinknecht, L-J.K. van den Scott, and C.B. Sanders. Toronto, ON: Canadian Scholars' Press.

Vidich, Arthur J. and Joseph Bensman. 1958. *Small Town in Mass Society: Class, Power, and Religion in a Rural Community*. Champaign, IL: University of Illinois Press.

Viel, Matthew D. 2001. "Covenantal Ethics: A Living System for Living Systems." MA thesis, Loma Linda University.

Volkman, Toby A. 1990. "Visions and Revisions: Toraja Culture and the Tourist Gaze." *American Ethnologist* 17(1):91–110.

von Unger, Hella, Hansjörg Dilger, and Michael Schönhuth. 2016. "Ethikbegutachtung in der sozial- und kulturwissenschaftlichen Forschung? Ein Debattenbeitrag aus soziologischer und ethnologischer Sicht [Ethics Review in Social and Cultural Science Research? A Sociological and Anthropological Contribution to the Debate]." *Forum Qualitative Sozialforschung/Forum: Qualitative Social Research* 17(3):1–12.

Wallraff, Günter. 1985. *Ganz Unten*. Cologne, Germany: Kiepenheuer and Witsch.

Wax, Murray L. 1977. "On Fieldworkers and Those Exposed to Fieldwork: Federal Regulations and Moral Issues." *Human Organization* 33(3):321–28.

Whitney, Simon N. 2012. "The Python's Embrace: Clinical Research Regulation by Institutional Review Boards." *Pediatrics* 129(3):576–78.

Whitney, Simon N. and Carl E. Schneider. 2011. "Viewpoint: A Method to Estimate the Cost in Lives of Ethics Board Review of Biomedical Research." *Journal of Internal Medicine* 269(4):396–402.

Wojciechowska, Magdalena. 2018. "Doing Research on Behind-the-Scenes Phenomena: Entering the Female Escort Industry." Pp. 133–43 in *The Craft of Qualitative Research: A Handbook,* edited by S.W. Kleinknecht, L-J.K. van den Scott, and C.B. Sanders. Toronto, ON: Canadian Scholars' Press.

Woodward, Comer Vann. 1974. *Report of the Committee of Freedom of Expression at Yale*. New Haven, CT: Yale College.

Wright, Justin. 2018. "Using a Qualitative Approach in Applied Military Personnel Research." Pp. 107–13 in *The Craft of Qualitative Research: A Handbook,* edited by S.W. Kleinknecht, L-J.K. van den Scott, and C.B. Sanders. Toronto, ON: Canadian Scholars' Press.

Wynn, Lisa L. 2011. "Ethnographers' Experiences of Institutional Ethics Oversight: Results from a Quantitative and Qualitative Survey." *Journal of Policy History* 23(1):94–114.

Wynn, Lisa L. 2016. "What Is Wrong with Ethics Review, the Impact on Teaching Anthropology, and How to Fix It: Results of an Empirical Study." *Australian Journal of Anthropology* 28(3):269–85.

Yanow, Dora and Peregrine Schwartz-Shea. 2018. "Framing 'Deception' and 'Covertness' in Research: Do Milgram, Humphreys, and Zimbardo Justify Regulating Social Science Research Ethics?" *Forum Qualitative Sozialforschung/Forum: Qualitative Social Research* 19(3):Article 15.

Zerubavel, Eviatar. 2006. *The Elephant in the Room: Silence and Denial in Everyday Life*. Oxford, UK: Oxford University Press.

Zywicki, Todd J. 2007. "Institutional Review Boards as Academic Bureaucracies: An Economic and Experiential Analysis." *Northwestern University Law Review* 101(2):861–95.

# Index

Academia (website), 35
"academic ethnography" genre, 49–50
American Anthropological Association
    (AAA), 49, 52, 53–54, 55, 116n1
Andersen, Raoul R., 1
anonymity, 12, 23, 24, 39, 44, 48, 66,
    70–71
anthropology
    introduction, 19, 47
    "academic ethnography" and
        "manners and customs"
        genres, 49–50
    applied anthropology, 51–52
    ethics, engagement with, 12–13,
        47–49, 55–56
    ethics, history of, 50–55, 93, 95
    medical model, impacts on, 56
    participant observation, 79
audit culture
    introduction, 18–19, 21
    appeal and proliferation, 21–22, 26
    critiques of, 27–29
    vs. diversity, 22, 26–27
    governance and, 27
    research-ethics crisis and, 2, 34, 88
Australia, 54
    *National Statement on Ethical*
        *Conduct in Research Involving*
        *Humans* (1999), 72
authenticity, 5
(auto)ethnography, 8–9

Baez, Benjamin, 39
Baggini, Julian, 17, 45
Barth, Karl, 98
Becker, Howard S., 44, 62
*Belmont Report*, 75
Benedict, Ruth, 50
benefit, privileged over risk, 111
Berkman, Benjamin, 76
biomedical research-ethics framework.
    *See* medical research-ethics
    framework
Biswas, Subir, 52, 54–55
Blackstock, Cindy, 115n1
Blok, Anton, 53
Boas, Franz, 50
Bond, Tim, 77–78, 116n2
Boser, Susan, 22, 115n4
Bouësseau, Marie-Charlotte, 36
Brassington, Iain, 72, 85
Breen, Kerry, 72
Brydon-Miller, Mary, 101
Buck, Christopher, 95
Buckle, Jennifer L., 37
Bull, Julie, 4–5, 6–7, 8, 9, 10, 11
Burris, Scott, 78, 81

Canada, 83, 102. *See also* Indigenous
    research ethics; *Tri-Council*
    *Policy Statement* (TCPS);
    *Tri-Council Policy Statement 2*
    (TCPS 2)

## Index

Cannella, Gaile S., 76
capital-intensive research, 17, 34, 103
capture, 10, 31–32
Carpenter, Dale, 81–82
Castillo, Fatima Alvarez, 92
Castillo, Rosa Cordillera A., 86, 92, 93, 94–95, 100, 102, 104–05
Childress, Herb, 80
CITI (Collaborative Institutional Training Initiative), 113
Cloke, Paul, 85–86
Cohen, Anthony P., 1
Coleman, Carl H., 36
colonization, 10, 32–33, 108
Committee on Ethics of the International Preparatory Commission for the International Congress on Mental Health, 52
committees. *See* research-ethics committees
Common Rule, 76, 79, 116n1
communities, and research, 75–76, 111
compliance, 89, 93. *See also* audit culture
conferences, ethics-policy, 113–14
confidentiality, 12, 23, 24, 39–40, 44, 48, 71
conflict theory, 60
consent, informed
  anthropology and, 48, 79
  critiques of, 24, 40, 44, 46, 59, 70–71, 85, 88
  ethical "failures" and, 12
  Indigenous research ethics and, 111
  in medical model, 23
  situated ethics and, 77, 78
  tightened ethics codes, proposals for, and, 96

cooperative approaches, 59–60
Council of the European Union, 80–81
covenantal ethics, 97–99. *See also* research-ethics covenant
Cressey, Paul, 62
Cutcliffe, John, 78

Dalton, Melville, 62
DA-RT (Data Access and Research Transparency), 25
data and data sets, 24–25, 44
DeBruin, Debra, 75
deception, 12, 68
Department of Education (US), 17
de Sola Pool, Ithiel, 34–35
De Vries, Raymond, 75
dictation, 10, 32. *See also* colonization
digital culture and media, 17, 39
dignity, human, 71, 86
Dillman, Caroline, 52–53
Dingwall, Robert, 29, 85, 110–11
discovery research, 94
distress, physical or mental, 12
diversity, and audit culture, 22, 26–27
Dobrin, Lise, 79
doctor–patient relationship, 65
Dodds, Susan, 72
Dougherty, Debbie, 41–42, 43
Douglas, Jack, 62
Downie, Jocelyn, 83

Eckenwiler, Lisa A., 78
Edwards, Nichole, 88–89
Ehrenreich, Barbara, 63
Emmerich, Nathan, 85
ethics
  covenantal ethics, 97–99

ethical governance vs. professional ethics, 116n2
ethical space, 7, 11
ethics checklists, 89
ethics drift, 71 (*see also* mission creep)
ethics education, 71, 102, 104–05, 113
ethics-policy conferences, 113–14
vs. governance, 15
new ethics, 79–81
situated ethics, 77–79
vertical ethics, 112
*See also* medical research-ethics framework; research-ethics committees; research-ethics covenant; research-ethics review and regulation
Ethics Rupture Summit (2012), 108, 110, 117n7. See also *New Brunswick Declaration on Research Ethics, Integrity, and Governance*
*EthNav*, 48
ethnography, 8–9, 17, 37, 45–46, 56, 74, 79
*Etuaptmumk* (Two-Eyed Seeing), 7, 9
European Commission, 80

Fanon, Frantz, 32–33
Fine, Gary Alan, 25, 68
Fitzgerald, Maureen, 74
Foucault, Michel, 68
Fraser, Malcolm, 97
free speech, 68

gender, and research-ethics committees, 42

gender equality, 90–91
Germany, 38, 115n2
Gilpin, Adele M.K., 84
Goffman, Erving, 41, 43
  *Asylums*, 62, 64, 94
Goodgame, Andrew, 75
Gordon, Judith B., 77
governance, 15, 27
Gromen, Harald, 29
Gunsalus, C. Kristina, 82–84
Gunther, Katja, 39

Haggerty, Kevin, 74, 83, 116n6
harm, 19, 57–58, 60, 70–71, 77–78, 82
Hawthorne Studies, 62
health research, 15, 17–18
Hebden, Carl W., 84
Hedgecoe, Adam, 29, 116n2
Heggen, Kristin, 29
Helgeland, Ingebord, 44
Hilsen, Anne Inga, 99–100, 101
Hobbes, Thomas, 60
Holmwood, John, 26
Hughes, Everett C., 60
human dignity, 71, 86
humanism, radical, 60–62, 63
*Human Organization* (journal), 51
Human Relations School, 62
human rights, 110–11
human subjects, 22, 71
Humphreys, Laud
  *Tearoom Trade*, 57–58, 64
Husain, Abbar, 24

Indermaur, David, 46
India, 54
Indigenous, use of term, 115n1

Indigenous research ethics, 3–11
    introduction and author's
        background, 3–4
    (auto)ethnography and, 8–9
    Bull's approach, 4–5, 8
    challenges implementing, 9
    community consent and, 111
    components and impacts, 6–7
    medical model and, 10, 31
    reflexivity and, 7–8
    research-ethics covenant and, 5,
        9–11
    *Tri-Council Policy Statement
        (TCPS)* and, 5
    Truth and Reconciliation
        Commission's *Calls to Action*
        and, 5–6
individualistic vision of social life, 65–67
inductive research, 23, 37
informed consent. *See* consent, informed
institutional review boards (IRBs), 29,
        41, 75, 76, 83, 115n3. *See also*
        research-ethics committees
integrity, ethos of, 91–92
interdisciplinary research, 18, 26–27,
        29, 34
International Congress on Mental
        Health, Committee on
        Ethics of the International
        Preparatory Commission, 52
interview-based research, 24, 37, 45–46,
        56, 82
Iphofen, Ron, 14–15

Jennings, Sean, 72–73, 116n2
journalism, 63–64, 66, 86, 116n3
Juritzen, Truls, 29

Kleinknecht, Steven
    *The Craft of Qualitative Research*, 25
Kohn, Tamara, 28
Kramer, Michael, 41–42, 43

Lederman, Rena S., 37, 79
Lotich, Patricia, 28
Lowman, John, 29, 40
loyalty, 54
lying, 60–61

Machiavelli, Niccolò, 68
Maiter, Sarah, 22, 104
"manners and customs" genre, 49–50
Māori, 3, 101. *See also* Indigenous
    research ethics
marginalized groups, research on, 3, 67,
        70, 86
Marlowe, Jay, 75–76
Marshall, Albert, 7
Marshall, Murdena, 7, 115n2
Marxism, 60
Marzano, Marco, 19, 29, 90, 94. *See also*
    sociology
Mayo, Elton, 62
McWilliams, Rita, 84
medical research-ethics framework
    anonymity and, 12, 23, 24, 39, 44,
        48, 66, 70–71
    as capture and colonization, 10,
        31–33, 108
    capture by, history of, 33–35
    confidentiality and, 12, 23, 24,
        39–40, 44, 48, 71
    consent (*see* consent, informed)
    critiques of, 35–36, 37, 70–71,
        88–89

142

dominance of, 13–14, 21–22, 31,
    37–38
Indigenous research ethics and,
    10, 31
need to shift away from, 16–17, 18,
    22–23
vs. qualitative social research,
    16–17, 22–26, 57, 86
research-ethics crisis and, 2, 88
vulnerability and, 40, 70, 79, 108
*See also* research-ethics review and
    regulation
Méndez, Mariza, 8–9
mental or physical distress, 12
Mignone, Javier, 35
Milgram, Stanley, 64
mission creep, 83. *See also* ethics drift,
    *under* ethics
Mitchell, Richard G., 60
morality, 73, 98, 99. *See also* ethics

National Research Council of the
    National Academies, 116n1
*National Statement on Ethical Conduct
    in Research Involving
    Humans* (Australia, 1999), 72
Navajo, 98–99
neoliberalism, 17, 29, 73
*New Brunswick Declaration on
    Research Ethics, Integrity, and
    Governance*, 107–08, 110–14,
    115n5
new ethics, 79–81
New Zealand, 75–76
New Zealand Ethics Committee (NZEC),
    75–76
Nicholls, Stuart, 116n2

Nisbett, Richard E., 76
Nova Scotia attacks (2020), 90–91

Oakes, J. Michael, 75
Oakley, Ann, 88
Office for Human Research Protections
    (OHRP), 38, 93, 109–10
oral history, 82. *See also* interview-based
    research

Palys, Ted, 29, 40
Panel on Research Ethics, 15, 102
participant observation, 79
participatory action research, 71
Paul, Walter Joe, 4
Pels, Peter, 17, 49, 50, 52, 54
Perez, Teresa S., 77
physical or mental distress, 12
Poole, Roger, 7
Posel, Deborah, 76
positivist research, 17–18, 35
Power, Michael, 78
power dynamics, 42, 50, 53, 64–65,
    66–67, 103
Pratt, Marie Louise, 49
privacy, 12, 23, 55

Qualitative Analysis Conference, 24,
    115n1
qualitative social research
    cultural pressures on, 103–04
    ethics regulation and, 57, 58
    hurt perspective within, 35
    vs. medical models, 16–17, 22–26,
        57, 86
    objectives of, 23
    *Tri-Council Policy Statement 2*

Index

(TCPS 2) and, 15–16
See also anthropology; sociology
Quebec, 74, 116n6

radical humanism, 60–62, 63
Ramcharan, Paul, 78
Rashkover, Randi, 98
reciprocity, 103, 104
reflexivity and relationality, 7–8, 90, 98–100
researcher exemption (scholar's shield law), 73–74, 116n6
researcher–participant relationship, 24, 59–60, 65–66
research-ethics committees
    as consultant and vision keeper, 80
    critiques of, 36–38, 40–44, 89–90, 107, 109
    *New Brunswick Declaration*, 110, 112–13, 115n5
    and social science researchers, 45, 89, 117n9
    statistical data challenges, 115n3
    use of term, 115n3
    See also institutional review boards; research-ethics review and regulation
research-ethics covenant, 97–105
    introduction, 3, 19–20, 70, 86, 87
    covenantal ethics and, 97–99
    features and implications of, 91–92, 99–101, 103, 104–05
    implementation, 102, 105
    Indigenous research ethics and, 5, 9–11
research-ethics review and regulation
    introduction, 2–3, 11–12, 13–14, 18–20, 90, 95–97
    alternative models, challenges finding, 14–15, 93–94
    anonymity and, 12, 23, 24, 39, 44, 48, 66, 70–71
    anthropology and, 56
    author's background, 1–2
    as capture and colonization, 10, 31–33, 108
    centralization, proposal for, 84
    change, hopes for, 114
    changing mandate, 29
    confidentiality and, 12, 23, 24, 39–40, 44, 48, 71
    consent (*see* consent, informed)
    consequences for social research, 45–46
    cooperative approaches and, 59–60
    in crisis, 2, 88–90
    cultivating ethical awareness, 92, 94–95
    cultural influences on, 103–04
    debates, literature, and proposals, 35, 69–70, 71–72, 96, 108, 117nn2–4
    doing away with, proposals for, 84–86
    ethics drift and mission creep, 71, 83
    free speech and, 68
    governance vs. ethics, 15
    history of, 12–13
    individualistic vision of social life and, 65–67
    limiting the scope of, 79
    need to shift away from medical model, 16–17, 18, 22–23

*New Brunswick Declaration*,
    107–08, 110–14, 115n5
obligations, uneven disbursement
    of, 109–10
processes vs. practices, 14–15
radical humanism and, 60–62
rebalancing from within, proposals
    for, 73–81, 96
regulatory split among disciplines,
    proposals for, 81–84, 96
scholar's shield law (researcher
    exemption), 73–74, 116n6
situated ethics and, 77–79
social context of research (new
    ethics), 79–81
sociology's public relevance and,
    63–65
tightening current codes, proposals
    for, 72–73, 96
transparency, 26, 74–75
vertical ethics and, 112
vulnerability and, 40, 70, 79, 108
*See also* anthropology; audit
    culture; ethics; Indigenous
    research ethics; medical
    research-ethics framework;
    research-ethics committees;
    research-ethics covenant;
    sociology
ResearchGate, 35
Reynolds, Don, 103
risk, benefit privileged over, 111. *See also*
    harm
Roberts, Lynne, 46
Robinson, Perry, 98–99
Roger, Kerstin, 35
Rosenhan, David, 64

Ross, Fiona C., 76
Roy, Donald, 62
Russell, Cherry, 40
Ryan, Janice, 88

Salemink, Oscar, 49
Sartre, Jean-Paul, 32–33
Saviano, Roberto, 63
Scarce, Rik, 73
Scarth, Bonnie, 39
Scheper-Hughes, Nancy, 63
Schneider, Carl E., 28, 85
scholar's shield law (researcher
    exemption), 73–74, 116n6
Schrag, Zachary M., 84–85
    *Ethical Imperialism*, 34
secondary adjustment, 43
Shore, Cris, 28
Shore, Nancy, 75
Shulman, David, 61
Shweder, Richard A., 76
Sieber, Joan E., 64
Simmel, Georg, 60
situated ethics, 77–79
Smith, Linda Tuhiwai
    *Decolonizing Methodologies*, 6
snowball sampling, 44
social sciences. *See* qualitative social
    research; research-ethics
    review and regulation
Society of Applied Anthropology,
    51–52
sociology
    introduction, 19
    cooperative approaches and ethics
        regulation, 59–60
    ethics, history of, 12, 93, 95

*Index*

ethics regulation, consequences of, 57, 58
free speech and, 68
harm and, 57–58
individualistic vision of social life and, 65–67
interdisciplinarity and, 26–27, 29
public relevance, diminishing of, 63–65
radical humanism and ethics regulation, 60–62, 63
Solnit, Rebecca
*A Paradise Built in Hell*, 2
Stark, Laura M.
*Behind Closed Doors*, 34
Strathern, Marilyn, 28
students, 42, 93, 102, 104–05, 108, 113

Taylor, Alison, 36, 38, 41, 44
Tolich, Martin, 64, 75–76
Traianou, Anna, 68
transparency, 26, 74–75
Tri-Council Policy Statement (TCPS), 5, 6, 107
Tri-Council Policy Statement 2 (TCPS 2), 15–16, 109, 117n5
trust and trustworthiness, 5, 26, 41, 101
truth, misrepresenting, 60–61
Truth and Reconciliation Commission (TRC), *Calls to Action*, 5–6
Two-Eyed Seeing (*Etuaptmumk*), 7, 9

United Kingdom, 54
United States of America, 50, 52, 82–83, 93, 95. *See also* Common Rule; Department of Education; institutional review boards; Office for Human Research Protections
*Universal Declaration of Human Rights*, 110
University of Edinburgh, 27

Vainio, Annukka, 39
van den Hoonaard, Deborah K., 23, 25, 93
van den Scott, Jeffrey, 101
van den Scott, Lisa-Jo, 101
vertical ethics, 112
Viel, Matthew D., 98
virtue, 78
Volkman, Toby, 49
von Unger, Hella, 38
vulnerability, 40, 70, 79, 108

Wallraff, Günter, 63
Weber, Max, 60
Weeks, Peter, 89–90
Welsh, Jen, 78
Wong, Jan, 116n3
World Medical Association, 78–79

Yule, Elisa, 74

Zywicki, Todd, 77

Milton Keynes UK
Ingram Content Group UK Ltd.
UKHW030519301024
450418UK00004B/95